Mastering

Google Sites

Last updated: Jan 6 2025

HARRY SY JUNG

DEDICATION

To My Wife and My Son

TABLE OF CONTENTS

ACKNOWLEDGMENTS

Thanks to everyone who read the first draft of my iteration. Thanks also to Google and Google Sites team for making it possible for me to write Google Sites books.

CHAPTER 1 Understanding the Google Sites

Introduction

If you are looking for an easy way to create a website or an intranet for your business or organization, Google Sites is an ideal option. This powerful tool from Google allows you to quickly and easily create a robust website without needing any coding knowledge. With this book, you will be able to get started with Google Sites quickly and create a website that is perfect for your needs. Whether you are creating a portfolio website, a company intranet, or simply a place to showcase your work, Google Sites is easy to use and versatile enough to meet all your requirements.

What is Google Sites and Who Should Use It?

Google Sites is a free website builder that allows you to easily create and publish a professional website for your business or organization. You don't need any prior knowledge of website design or any special software to create a website. All you need is a web browser (preferably Google Chrome) with an internet connection and Gmail account, and you are good to go.

Google Sites is the best tool for information sharing and collaboration. If you want to create a website for your organization or business, but you don't want to deal with the hassle of installing, configuring, and maintaining a full-blown website, Google Sites is an ideal solution.

Something else that is great about Google Sites is that it is completely integrated with Google services so you can easily use your existing google tools and accounts. Furthermore, Google Sites is continually being improved by Google, so you can expect better functions and improvements on your next login.

Google Sites for your Business

Websites have become the de facto marketing and communication tool for many businesses. With the right Content Management System, or CMS, businesses can have their own branded websites at a low cost and easily manage their content.

Website builders such as WordPress, Drupal and Joomla are free to use and have a myriad of free and premium plugins available to extend their functionalities. However, these platforms do not provide a space for businesses to manage their content centrally, or to tailor communication and marketing efforts to target the right audience.

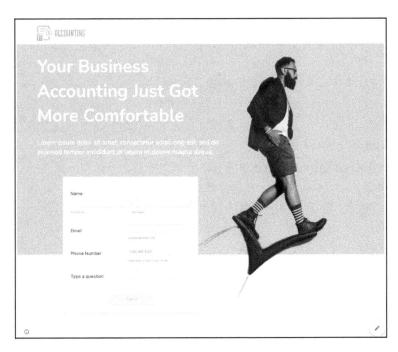

Figure 1.1

Figure 1.2

Figure 1.3

Google Sites is a free, easy-to-use website creator that allows you to create a site in a few simple steps from your desktop. Google Sites lets you build a professional-looking, fast, easy-to-manage site with the tools you need. You can also manage your content with built-in CMS and choose from a variety of free templates.

Google Sites for Schools and Non-Profit Organizations

Your school probably uses Google Workspace for Education to store student information, organize class documents, and facilitate collaboration. If you aren't using Google Sites as part of your integrated strategy, then you are missing out on some great benefits!

Google Sites is free for anyone who wants to use it. This makes it an ideal solution for schools, because it doesn't require any investment. It also means that your school doesn't have to worry about purchasing or maintaining servers. It does not consume any storage in your google drive, making it a cost-effective solution so your school can scale to meet its needs quickly and easily.

Figure 1.4

Google Sites allow people to collaboratively create and edit pages easily. The default style of Google Sites is very clean and minimalistic. This makes it easy for the school admin or non-profit committee to create and edit a page quickly. You can make the site look more like your class branding simply by adding your school's logo and colors. Google Sites also allow people to make their page "interactive". This means that they can embed YouTube videos, Google Calendars, Google Maps, and graphs into their page. This makes it easy to create a page that has both text and visual elements.

Google Sites also allow people to create links between pages. This means that you can create a page that links it to other pages.

By utilizing this function, your Google Site now becomes the central hub for information and collaboration. You can create pages that centralize important information, such as weekly class updates, events, curriculums and the school's policy on absences or sick leave. It can also mean that you can create pages that link to other pages where students can collaborate on projects and assignments and can be further linked to Google Classroom as well.

Non-profit organizations can build donation pages or community pages without hiring designers. It is super easy for volunteers to set up their non-profit organizations' websites with Google Sites and share to collaborate. Moreover, local governments can link to service websites from their homepage on Google Sites.

Figure 1.5

Figure 1.6

7 Key Features of Google Sites

I have been involved with hundreds of Google Sites projects and I've discovered some great features that all Google Sites fans would appreciate. Let's dive in.

1. Mobile friendly

First off, all of Google Sites web pages are automatically optimized for mobile screens on iPhones, Android devices, iPads, and Android tablets. You don't need to fine-tune your pages for mobile screens. Simply said, it will look great on any device.

2. Take advantage of 60+ Google services

Google Sites is built by Google. Therefore, you can embed all kinds of Google services, such as YouTube, Google Docs, Google Slides, Google Sheets, Google Drive, Google Forms, Google Maps, and Google Groups in a few clicks.

3. Embed Javascript, widgets and even webpage as a full page.

In addition, you can use the HTML embed feature to embed widgets from other websites like Jotform, Elvesight, Twitter, and Facebook, among others. Plus, Google Sites lets you embed any content and website as a full page.

4. Built-in contents management system

One of the best features of Google Sites is its built-in CMS, or content management system. You can see revision histories and revert to previous versions if you or your colleagues accidentally altered the content. This is especially helpful if you need to review or see how your website evolved.

5. Site access permission control to internal folks

Did you know that Google Sites is a popular intranet platform? You can build an intranet website for your organization, department, or team and then share it to your stakeholders. You may give readers permission to view the page, while editors may edit and maintain it for better collaboration.

6. Custom theme

When it comes to theme, creating a custom Google Sites theme is as simple as designing a Google Slides presentation. You can use your brand's identity, color scheme, and background images to customize your Google Sites theme. Creating a theme or entire Google sites is simple with Google Sites. You can replicate a theme or even an entire Google site in a couple of clicks. You can build on top of one of the free available Google Sites themes or buy a custom Google Sites design from experts.

7. Unlimited possibilities

Google Sites is a free website builder and super easy to use. There is no hosting cost or storage taken off your Google Drive. Google Sites can be anything from websites to cloud storage, bookmarks, linktree, and even hosted web applications on different platforms, opening up unlimited possibilities.

Google Sites and Content Management System

Google Sites has a built-in content management system (CMS) that lets you see revision histories and revert to previous versions. This is convenient because content management systems help you control your site. It means having the ability to update, change or delete any images, text, video or audio — really anything at all! And it's so easy and organized, too. You can restore a single page or an entire site. Here's how.

How to restore a page

Step 1. Hover to the 'Three Dot' menu icon on the top right corner of your Google Sites and select the first option 'version history' from the drop-down options.

Step 2. You will see the list of versions of the site on the right sidebar: choose the version you wish to restore.

Step 3. On top of the page, click the 'Restore this page version' button.

Step 4. The Google Sites will ask you if you want to restore this version: click 'Restore page' if it's the right version; click 'Cancel' if it's the wrong one. You will be notified that the page has been restored by Google Sites.

Figure 1.7

Figure 1.8

How to revert to the previous version of a Google Sites.

Step 1. Hover to the 'Three Dot' menu icon on the top right corner of your Google Sites and select the first option 'Version history' from the drop down options.

Step 2. Choose the version of your site that you want to restore and revert to from the list of versions.

Step 3. Choose 'Restore this version' button > click 'Restore' and the site will restore that version of the site. Version history preserves all revisions of the site after the version you restore to, so you won't lose those changes and can revert back to those revisions at any time.

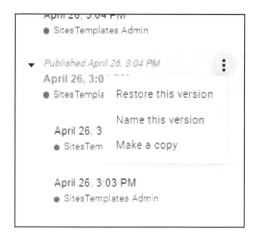

Figure 1.9

Figure 1.10

How to Restore Deleted Content of Google Sites

Step 1. Hover to the 'Three Dot' menu icon on the top right corner of your Google Sites and select the first option 'Version history' from the drop-down options.

Step 2. Look for the version of your site that contains the deleted content you want to restore.

Step 3. Click the 'Three Dot' button next to the version name/date on the right.

Step 4. Make a copy of the site at that time by selecting the 'Make a copy' option.

Step 5. Copy the deleted content from this version and paste it into the original site.

Name your own version in Google Sites

If you prefer, you can name a version of the new Google site any name you want. Click the 'Three Dot' button in the version list page and choose "Name this version", then enter the name you want for the site version.

5 Common Mistakes to Avoid When Creating Google Sites

Building a website on Google Sites can be an exciting endeavor, but it's easy to overlook crucial elements during the process. Paying attention to the details can make a significant difference in creating a successful and SEO-friendly website. In this blog, we will explore the five most common mistakes people make when crafting Google Sites and provide valuable tips on how to avoid them, ensuring that your website stands out from the competition.

1. Favicon

Often overlooked, the favicon is a small yet powerful element of your website. It appears in the browser's tab or address bar and helps visitors recognize and remember your brand. Additionally, when users bookmark your website, the favicon is displayed next to the link. But that's not all! Search engines may also showcase your favicon alongside your website's title and meta description in search results. A well-designed favicon can leave a lasting impression, so don't underestimate its importance.

Tip: Create a simple and eye-catching favicon that reflects your brand identity for better recognition.

2. Short Links and Footer Menus

While a navigation bar in the header is essential, many forget about the footer. It's just as important! The footer allows you to add resource links and short links, providing users with convenient navigation options throughout your website. Having well-organized and accessible menus in the footer can enhance user experience and encourage visitors to explore more of your content.

Tip: Categorize your footer menus appropriately and ensure that they complement the header navigation for a seamless browsing experience.

3. Mobile Responsiveness

With an increasing number of users accessing websites on their mobile devices, having a mobile-responsive design is non-negotiable. Google Sites offers a native mobile-friendly look and feel, saving you the trouble of designing a separate mobile version. However, it's essential to ensure that your chosen design looks appealing and functions flawlessly on mobile and tablets.

Tip: Regularly preview your website on various mobile devices to ensure optimal user experience across different screen sizes.

4. Social Icons

In the current digital era, having a strong social media presence is essential for both businesses and individuals. Integrating social icons on your Google Sites website allows visitors to connect with your brand across various platforms. Don't forget to include links to your blog and other relevant affiliate pages to further engage your audience and expand your online community.

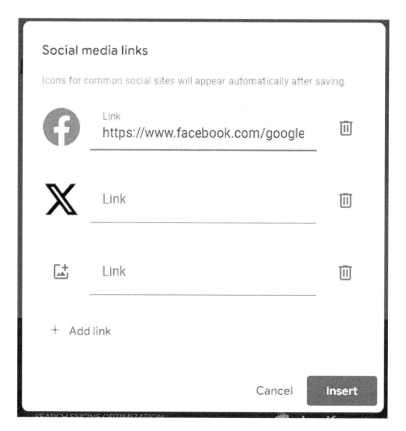

Tip: Use prominent social icons that match your website's design and place them in a visible spot on the footer for easy access.

5. Google Analytics

Building a website is just the first step; understanding your audience and their behavior is vital for its success. Google Analytics offers valuable insights on website traffic and user interactions. By integrating Google Analytics with your Google Sites, you can track the performance of your site, identify areas for improvement, and make data-driven decisions to boost conversions and enhance user engagement.

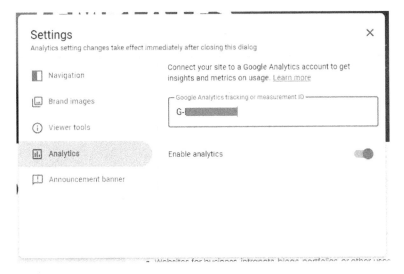

Tip: Set up Google Analytics early in the website creation process to monitor your site's performance from the beginning.

Google Sites for Intranet

An intranet is a private network that lets employees share information. It's like a company's own portal, and helps communicate updates and news to all staff at once. Companies use it to create their own internal social and collaborative networks instead of relying on outside sources for communication.

If your company is looking for a solution to build a private, secure intranet, Google Sites is one of the best options. It's inexpensive and easy to create, and it comes with all the features of a full-fledged intranet service. I'll explain why you should choose Google Sites as your solution for building an intranet.

Affordable and Simple

Google Sites is a great choice if you're on a tight budget and need to prioritize simplicity. Google Sites comes with all the features of other expensive solutions. Anyone involved in your business can become a collaborator and admin on Google Sites by sharing their email address.

Security and Efficiency

Often, the need for an intranet is driven by a need for security. For example, your company needs to protect sensitive information or limit access to certain users. You should choose Google Sites because it's free and easy to use, plus there are no fees for adding new staff users or updating content.

In addition, since Google Sites is secured by Google Cloud, your data is more secure than with other intranet services. With this service, you don't have to worry about having unprotected content on the internet anymore. It also comes with all of the features of other expensive solutions so there's never a question of not being able to do what you need to do with your intranet service.

Google Sites is perfect for small businesses who want an inexpensive solution for their digital transformation efforts without sacrificing quality or security. Your company will receive all of the benefits of an expensive service without any of the costs associated with them.

Scalable and Customizable

Google Sites is scalable, meaning that you can start out with a simple site and then add more features as you need them. You don't have to start from scratch — Google Sites will grow with your business.

In addition, Google Sites is customizable so you can change the color scheme to match your company's style or build a mobile-friendly website. It's an easy solution for building a site from scratch.

Digital Transformation

Digital transformation is an increasingly popular buzzword in the business world. What does it mean? The definition of digital transformation varies depending on who you ask. However, most agree that it's a combination of integrating new technologies into your company to improve customer experience and operations.

Some companies are taking this step by investing in digital marketing to build their online presence. And while some marketing strategies, like pay-per-click (PPC) advertising, are entirely outsourced, Search Engine Optimization, or SEO isn't one of them. Why? Because SEO is still too complex for freelancers to handle on their own.

As a small business, you don't have time for complicated web design or finding out how search engines work. That's why outsourcing SEO is the best option for most companies.

Do You Need Google Workspace for Google Sites?

Google Sites available in free Gmail as well as Google Workspace as part of Google Service. For the free Gmail account, you can use Google Sites without paying any license fees. Furthermore, it does not have a storage limit or a bandwidth limit. This website builder is perfect for small businesses and startups.

What about Google Workspace for Google Sites?

Now, you may wonder if Google Workspace is necessary for Google Sites. With Google Workspace, you get business email, Google Docs, and Drive with a minimum of 30GB storage per user. Besides, it comes with Google's dedicated support, so you can send an email or chat for assistance for Google Sites. If you're interested in learning more, contact our Google Workspace partner Gear Cloud Solutions (gearcs.com) and mention our book for a discount.

Feature Comparison and Support

On Google Sites, there's no functional difference between the one from personal Gmail and the one from Google Workspace. There is one key difference, however, and that is the ability to get troubleshooting and support.

Google Workspace includes Google Sites as one of its core services. You can contact Google Support directly whether you have an issue with Google Sites or want to take advantage of the Google Sites tips. Depending on your project, it may be worth your time and money.

Do I need a custom domain for Google Sites?

Google sites can be built without a business domain. The default URL for Google Sites is sites.google.com. To reserve your google sites URL, enter a unique name, such as sites.google.com/view/yourbusinessname.

It is also important to note that many scammers build phishing sites with sites.google.com, so some social media sites and other website networks consider sites.google.com to be a phishing or spam site.

For this reason, you need a domain name for your project, brand, or business. It costs just around $12 per year to register the domain. Your Google Sites can be connected to your domain once you buy it. A detailed explanation of how to connect your domain to Google Sites can be found in the next chapter.

Google Sites Advantages vs. Other platforms

Although there are many website builders out there with many advantages over Google Sites, I'll focus on why Google Sites is better than the others.

The advantages of Google Sites over WordPress

Google Sites is an alternative to WordPress for websites that are simple, organized and easy to manage. Google Sites is a free web-authoring tool from Google, available as part of Google Apps.

Because it's part of Google Apps, you don't need a domain name or hosting to set up your site (you can of course add a domain to Google Sites as well). You can create sites with content stored in Google Drive. Users can access your website on any device and see it how they want by viewing its mobile version.

You can also make this as a private site and invite your team, partners or customers so the site is accessible to authorized individuals only. With such benefits, it isn't surprising that many businesses have switched over from WordPress to Google Sites instead.

A major reason to consider Google Sites instead of WordPress is cost. WordPress.com is free, but if you want to use self-hosted WordPress software, you'll need to purchase a web hosting. Depending on the type of hosting you choose and the amount of traffic you consume, hosting costs can range from a few dollars to thousands of dollars per year. In contrast, Google Sites is completely free hosting to use.

You can also get more out of each Google Site than you can out of each WordPress site. Each Google Site can accommodate highest security, unlimited storage and bandwidth, thanks to Google Drive and Google's data centers globally.

Besides the cost, there are other reasons as well. Here are some of Wordpress' biggest drawbacks.

- Difficult to maintain: It is difficult to design, develop, and maintain WordPress websites if you aren't familiar with coding.
- Plugins, Themes: You would need to get design templates for better design and install lots of plugins for certain functionalities. Most of these efficiency-enhancing features and tools have a price. The more of them you use, the higher the cost of using WordPress goes.

- Frequent updates: Installing WordPress alone isn't enough. In order for it to work properly, you must install various plugins and themes. The more plugins you add, the more compatibility issues you will face, as well as loading time delays.

- Website vulnerability: It is a challenge to keep WordPress secure.. It is difficult because it relies heavily on plugins developed by different people, which increases the likelihood of malicious code infiltrating its functionalities.

- Poor SEO: It can be difficult for people with no SEO experience to ensure the SEO friendliness of WordPress. If the content is divided into many categories or excessively tagged in WordPress, Google will flag it as duplicate content. This will significantly affect your site's SERP rankings.

The Advantages of Google Sites over Wix

Google Sites is a free and easy-to-use website builder from Google. It's great for beginner webmasters with limited time, resources, and knowledge. But why is Google Sites better than Wix? Here are top 6 reasons why Google Sites is the best option for building your website.

Google Sites is free hosting. Period. If you're a beginner webmaster who has limited time and resources, then your best option is Google Sites. It's free for anyone and offers the similar features as other website builders- but without the cost.

Meanwhile, you will pay at least $15 per month (notice annual billing vs. month-to-month pay) for hosting, and the price will increase as soon as you discover that there are limitations on bandwidth, contact forms, and freemium plugins.

No messy drag-and-drop components: The drag-and-drop components on Google

Sites is a great feature because it lets you build your website without having to know code. You'll be able to visually drag and drop elements onto the page, edit text, create links, upload images, and more. This means you don't have to spend hours learning or implementing coding languages such as HTML.

With Wix they do have many components and are easy to use, however, whenever you want to add something, you need to add a Strip or manually adjust the height to make the room, and it can become quite messy when components overlap or some anomaly happens (i.e. repeaters are almost never consistent). If you encounter any unexpected problems, you may need to contact Wix support.

Google Sites has no inconsistencies on mobile responsive design. You may not think about your website's responsiveness when you're designing it, but this is one of the most important parts of building a website. What if you want to bring in new users who access their websites on their mobile phone? Almost half of website traffic comes from mobile devices these days, and with that statistic, it's clear that having a responsive design is crucial.

Obviously, Wix is great, but the biggest drawback is that the design on desktop is not consistent on mobile. You should always check whether your website is displaying well on mobile whenever you make changes in the editor. Just because it looks good on desktop doesn't mean it will look good on mobile.

In Google Sites, you don't have to worry about mobile view inconsistency. It's truly auto-resizable and displays well on mobile devices.

Security and accessibility: Google Sites is a web builder, which means the website you build with it will be hosted on Google's servers. This offers security and accessibility for beginners.

With a Wix site, the hosting and domain are handled by Wix, meaning you'll have less control about who has access to your files and how secure your files are. As a beginner webmaster, this should be an important feature that you want to look for in a builder like Google Sites.

Unlimited Bandwidth: Google Sites does not have a bandwidth limit. Google Sites are hosted by dozens of Google data centers worldwide, come with Gmail, and, guess what, their speed should be fast as there are 1.5 billion Gmail users and millions of Google Workspace domains.

You can create an unlimited amount of pages, photos, and videos with Google Sites. This means that you don't have to worry about your website being slow or crashing if too many people go to it at once.

Meanwhile, you will have to spend a lot of money to make your website load quickly from Wix. You don't want your website rank to be affected by poor loading speed on search engines.

Google Search friendly: One of the best features of Google Sites is that it's search-engine-friendly. Search engines like Google and Bing rank well-optimized pages higher than those that are not well optimized. With Google Sites, you can create a website with SEO in mind. This will help it rank higher on search engine results pages for specific keywords or phrases related to your company.

Disclaimer

It is true that Google Sites has a lot of limits, but depending on the needs of your project and/or budget, you may want to choose Google Sites over Wix, Wordpress or other website builders.

Side note: You can get dedicated support from Google for your Google Sites if you purchase Google Workspace. For Google Sites with a personal Gmail — you can check Google Sites community pages for support.

CHAPTER 2 Getting Started with Google Sites

Now that you have a pretty good understanding of Google Sites, it's time to get started with your new website project.

Setting Up Your Google Sites Account

Before you start creating your website, you need to first set up your Gmail account. Gmail is totally free for personal use and can sign up via Gmail.com. You would need a cell phone to complete the signing up process.

If you would like further instructions on setting up a Gmail account, please visit the Gmail website at Gmail.com and follow the latest step-by-step instructions.

Creating New Website in Google Sites

If you already have a Gmail account, then you can login to Google Sites using the same credentials. Here's how to do it:

Step 1. Log in to your Google account at https://sites.google.com

Step 2. You can start a new site by clicking blank (+ in a box) or choose from the free templates in the gallery. Alternatively, you can buy nice design templates at https://sitestemplates.net if you want some awesome design templates.

Customizing your Google Sites

Once your website is created, you can start adding content to it. Google Sites starts with the default website URL starting at https://sites.google.com/... and this is your editing mode URL and the site is not yet published.

Figure 2.1

User Interface

In your Google Sites editing mode, there are three sections. In the top sections, you'll find Sites name, Undo/Redo, mobile and desktop view modes, sharing, settings, and version history, as well as options to copy and publish.

Secondly, the body section represents your website, and you can add contents to it. Last but not least, all components, pages, and themes are represented in the right sidebar.

Adding contents and components are pretty straight forward. Under the 'Insert' menu pane, you can find four types of contents: Text, Images, Embed or Drive.

- Text: Add text based contents under the text box.
- Images: Add images to the site.
- Embed: Embed html and javascript code within the site.
- Drive: Choose files from your Google Drive and embed within the site.

When you double-click on Google Sites body, you will notice a circle with options such as Embed, Images, Text, Upload, and From Drive.

- Content Blocks: You can click to add layouts like two columns and four columns.

- Additionally, you can add many components within Google Sites, such as buttons, image carousels, social links, YouTube videos, and Google Calendars.

Navigation, Header and Footer Design Best Practices

All websites have three major sections. The header, body, and footer. The header and footer are equally important as the body, and making them stand out will create an everlasting impression. I'll show you how to make it stand on Header and Footer in Google Sites.

Google Sites Navigation & Header: It's no secret that your website's header can make or break your business's success. A great header will draw in visitors, encourage them to explore your site, and make a lasting impression.

Navigation: Navigation is always the first thing that appears on Google Sites. You will notice the gear icon when you move your cursor to the top area of the Google Sites. When you click on the 'Gear' icon, you'll see the option to show the navigation bar on the 'Top' or 'Side'. Whenever you view your Google Sites on a mobile device, your navigation bar always appears as a sidebar.

Figure 2.2

In Navigation settings, you can do the following.

- View mode: Top/Side (Mobile always shows Side due to screen size)

- Brand images: You can upload a logo and a favicon here. Your favicon and logo can also be uploaded in 'Themes'.
- Viewer tools: The Info icon and Anchor links can be turned on or off.
- Analytics: You can enable analytics and connect your Google Analytics account
- Announcement banner: Display the banner along with the announcement bar's message, label, and link at the top of your website.

The logo height is incorporated into the top navigation bar height, so it may be disappointingly small. If this is the case, I recommend uploading the logo in the header area.

Header

Google Sites Header: Mouse hover over the header area (just below the top navigation bar) and you will notice a small bar with three options: 'Change Image', 'Reset', and 'Header Type' as well as two symbols representing 'Remove readability adjustment' and 'Anchor image'.

- Change Image: You can change the header's main background image. In addition to the sample photo galleries on Google Sites, you can upload images from your computer, Dropbox, Google Drive, or add them by URL.
- Reset: If you want to return to the original state, you can always reset.
- Header type: You can choose either a large cover background or a small banner background, depending on your needs. You can choose 'Title only' if you do not need a background image for your header

Figure 2.3

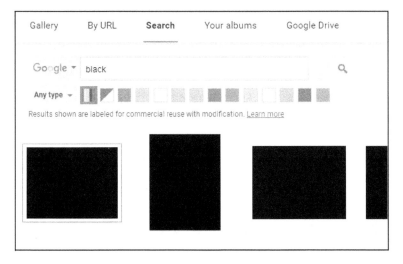

Figure 2.4

Tip: If you want a solid color as your header background, you don't need to make an image. You can search for images on Google and choose from them.

- Remove readability adjustment: You can adjust background image color for better readability of text.
- Anchor image: By choosing the position of the arrow, you can highlight a specific area in your background image.

In order to embed an image on the header, double-click the mouse button or go to Insert > Images on the right sidebar to upload an image such as your logo on top of the header background. When you double click the mouse button and choose an image, you can't upload an image from your computer. In this case, go to the right side bar and choose 'Images' to upload your image from your computer.

Figure 2.5

Google Sites Footer: Website footers are often overlooked, but they are an essential part of any website design. Footers are the last thing visitors see on a page and can be used to draw attention to key information, such as contact information, copyright notices, legal disclaimers, social icons and more. They also provide a way to link visitors to other pages within your site. When designed correctly, a footer can be an effective way to boost engagement and make your website more user-friendly.

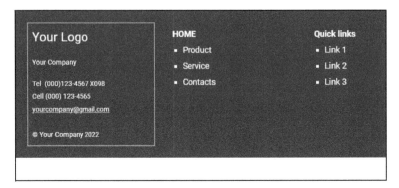

Figure 2.6

To create a strong footer, you can add a text box with bullet points to organize your menu links. Plus, displaying a logo and social media icons will draw attention. Lastly, you can include a section in the footer for subscribers or promotional banners.

It is possible to replicate a section and then pick a palette to switch the background color or add an image. Ultimately, you can create something similar to this.

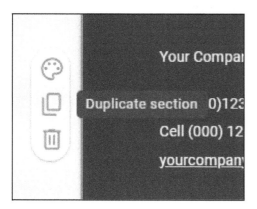

Figure 2.7

Figure 2.8

Adjust Margin Wherever You Want with Spacer Option in Google Sites

In case you're stuck due to margin limitations in Google Sites, here's good news for you! The spacer feature in Google Sites allows you to have a more flexible margin between image and text sections. Having this option makes designing a webpage much easier for web designers.

In Google Sites, you can select Compact, Cozy, or Comfortable spacing from Custom Themes, but this option isn't available if you select default themes like Simple, Aristotle, or Diplomat.

With spacer, you can adjust margins on any page in any section. Here's how.

Whenever you need to add a spacing, go to the Insert menu panel and select 'Spacer' option.

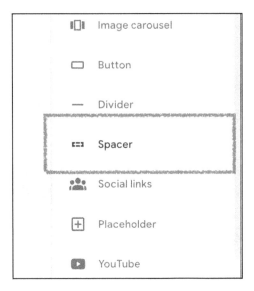

Figure 2.9

Dotted rectangles indicate spacing. Simply hover your mouse over the margin and adjust it.

Figure 2.10

Of course, custom themes can be used for the above spacing options as well as spacers for any sections.

Three Ways to Upload and Store Images in Google Sites.

When you create a new Google Sites, it is automatically saved to your Google Drive. Yes, your entire website in Google is treated as a file and can be shared just like other documents that are found on google drive.

Google Sites has no storage limit, and Drive doesn't count any storage, so you can upload as many images or text to your Google Site as you like without worrying about it consuming your Drive space.

You should also take into account where your images are stored, and be able to export them when revision is needed.

When uploading images in Google Sites you need to consider the Pros and Cons that come with these three options.

Figure 2.11

Option 1. Add images from your computer to Google Sites

You can upload any number of files within your Google Sites and it will not count towards storage in your Drive. To upload images to your site, go to the 'Insert' pane on the right side of Google Sites editing page. From there you can select "Images" > "Upload" and select files from your computer.

Pros & Cons:

- Pros: You won't have to worry about storage.
- Cons: Hard to locate uploaded files. You may use the "Save Image As" option to download some of the images. However, if you want to extract a background image from your photo, that function does not exist and will be difficult to locate.

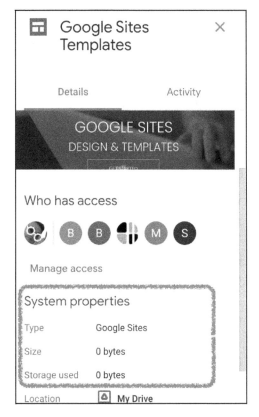

Figure 2.12

Option 2. Add images from your Google Drive to Google Sites

You can instead upload image files from your Google Drive. This is the easiest way to add to your google sites.

To add images to your site, go to the 'Insert' pane on the right side of Google Sites editing page. From there you can select "Images" > "Select" and select file from your Google Drive file list.

Pros & Cons:
- Pros: It's easy to find the files and it is easy to reuse them.
- Cons: Your image file will use Google Drive space.

Option 3. Add images by URL to Google Sites

To add images to your site, go to the 'Insert' pane on the right side of Google Sites editing page. From there you can select "Images" > "Select" and choose 'By URL' to enter the image link.

Pros & Cons:
- Pros: It won't consume your drive storage, and you can use external websites to host images.
- Cons: If the image you added to your website redirects and they remove it, it will be reflected on your site. If you use Google Drive Universal Link for image hosting, it will consume your drive storage.

Side Note: What is Google Drive Universal Link? First, share the image file with anyone with a link to view. And then find the fileID and use this link format:
https://drive.google.com/uc?export=view&id={fileID} For example, the image link below has a fileID of '1FelKrywVCfIZ5XJlrBxeG6KzfPz7q3Sz'.

Then google drive url is as follows:
https://drive.google.com/file/d/1FelKrywVCfIZ5XJlrBxeG6KzfPz7q3Sz/view?usp=sharing

To view your image on the web as universal lin, change the url as follows;
https://drive.google.com/uc?export=view&id=1FelKrywVCfIZ5XJlrBxeG6KzfPz7q3Sz

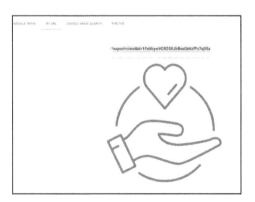

Figure 2.13

Mobile-First Indexing and Google Sites

In the ever-evolving digital landscape, Google's transition to mobile-first indexing marks a significant milestone, emphasizing the paramount importance of mobile-friendly websites. With the majority of internet traffic now originating from mobile devices, businesses and individuals cannot afford to overlook the impact of mobile optimization on their SEO performance.

Google's decision to prioritize mobile versions of websites stems from the undeniable dominance of smartphones and tablets in internet usage. As of July 2023, mobile devices account for over 63% of all global internet traffic, surpassing desktop usage for years. This shift in user behavior necessitates a corresponding shift in web development strategies.

Websites that fail to adapt to the mobile-first paradigm risk significant disadvantages in search rankings. Conversely, websites that provide a seamless and engaging mobile experience stand to reap substantial benefits, including improved rankings, increased visibility, and enhanced brand perception.

The good thing about Google Sites is that you don't have to build a different design or layout for mobile. Contents and components that you created on desktop are automatically optimized and resized for mobile devices. No need to worry about messy looks on mobile screens.

How to Publish Your Google Sites

Once you are done creating your website, you need to publish it. Click the [Publish] button on your upper right corner and enter the public name of the site. It will become your permanent google site name under sites.google.com default link.

Once you decide your public site name, you can connect this site URL to your actual domain.

When publishing Google Sites, why do you need to add a custom domain?

Globally, there are almost 1 million Google Sites. They are widely used due to their ease of use, integration with Google services, security and Google search friendliness. Many corporations use google sites internally or publicly as an intranet and some governments built entire websites on Google Sites.

As Google Sites is a native platform with reliable name authority and easy to use, some bad actors use them for phishing. A number of news articles report that scammers create websites with Google Sites to lure phishing sites.

This type of site can be found in Google Sites. This is a typical phishing website.

Figure 2.14

Because of this, some social media platforms miscategorize sites.google.com as phishing sites and mistakenly label you as a scammer.

To prevent this, there is a very simple solution. You can add a custom domain to your sites.google.com account

Site Note: How to report phishing Google Sites: The good news is that if you happen to come across a phishing site built using Google Sites, you can directly report it to Google, so that bad actors such as these have no place to hide. In order to report, there are two options:

>Option 1: Scroll down Google Sites and find the (!) circle on the left side. Click 'Report abuse' to report the scam site. To complete the report, you must choose one of the categories 'Spam, malware, or phishing'.
>Option 2: Report phishing attacks through Google's official website "Prevent & report phishing attacks" page.

Your Ultimate Guide to Setting Up a Custom Domain on Google Sites

How to add a domain to Google Sites is one of the most commonly asked questions, as well as one of the most daunting tasks. I will explain how to easily add a custom domain to your site.

Add your domain to Google Sites and verify

The first step is to add a custom domain directly to your Google sites. Go to your Google Sites and click the Gear icon (settings). In the Settings pop-up, select 'Custom domains'. You will only be able to see this 'Custom domains' menu option if you are the site owner. To add a domain, click the 'Add' button.

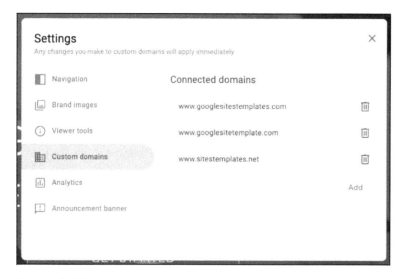

Figure 2.15

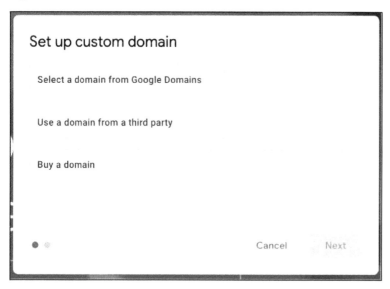

Figure 2.16

If you have a domain registered with Google Domains, you will be asked to login. You can then select a domain and the DNS records will be automatically added.

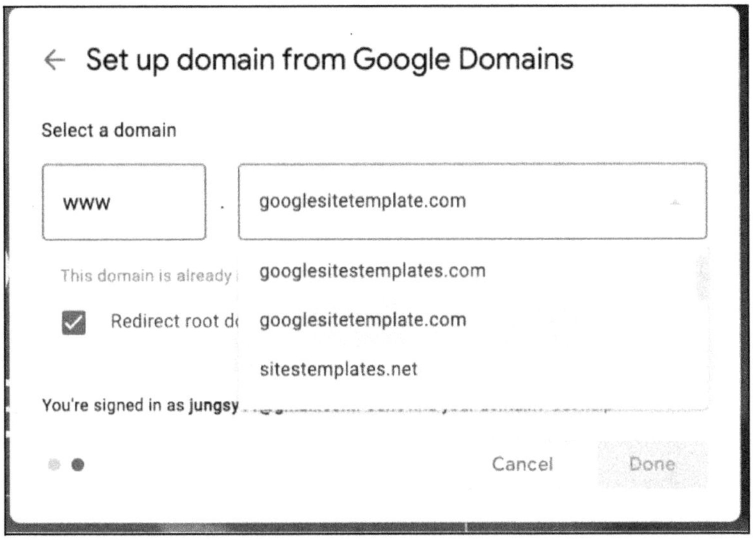

Figure 2.17

If you own your domain through a third party registrar, like GoDaddy, enter the domain and click the 'verify ownership' link. In your GoDaddy DNS manager, you would need to enter the TXT/CNAME record. Once records have been added and saved, click the 'VERIFY' button.

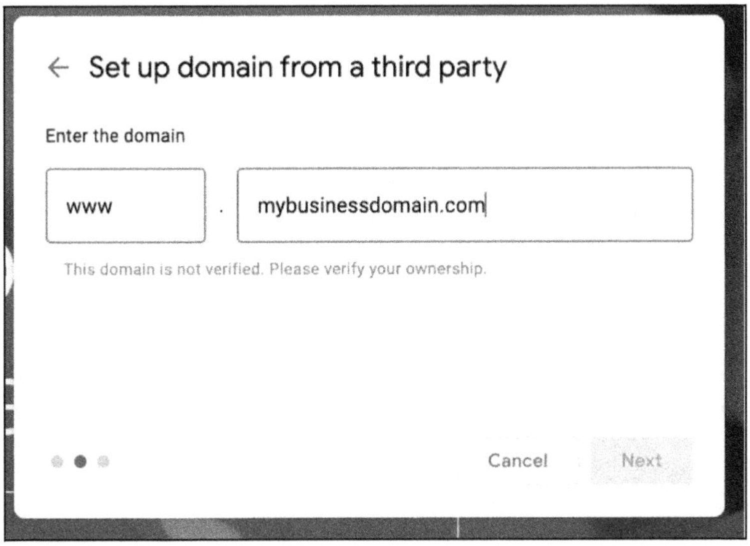

Figure 2.18

Figure 2.19

Don't forget Google Search Console

Your domain must be connected to Google Search Console in order to be verified. Select 'Add property' from the navigation pane.

It may seem redundant, but connecting to Google Search Console is the best and fastest way to connect your domain to Google sites. In addition, it will help you with your SEO efforts.

Google Search Console is a free tool offered by Google. It's a great way to make sure your website is running smoothly and that you're getting the most out of engaging with potential customers.

Google Search Console offers insights into how your site is performing in search engine results. It also provides information about any website errors, such as 404 pages, and crawling errors, such as robots.txt problems. In addition to diagnostics for your website, it offers insights on how other sites are linking to you.

You can find out what other websites have been mentioning your company and clicking on your links so you know where other people are finding you online!

Yes, Google Search Console does require a bit of technical knowledge if you want to really take advantage of all its features. However, it's still fairly easy to learn and use even if you don't have any prior knowledge about SEO or web analytics. If you're ready to start using Google Search Console today, check out this helpful guide!

Why Should You Be Using Google Search Console?

It can be difficult to get your web pages indexed by search engine crawlers. This is where Google Search Console comes in handy. It's a free tool that helps you identify any errors with your website, including problems with your site's code and content.

You also have access to insights about how people interact with your website and its pages. You see what users are clicking on, what they don't like, and more.

Google Search Console will help you find out if there are any issues with your site that would cause it to rank poorly in the search engines. That way, you can fix these issues and improve your site's ranking without having to pay for additional SEO services outside of Google Search Console.

It can also help you analyze performance data for specific keywords so you know which ones are most relevant for your business and which ones should receive more attention.

Google Search Console also offers a variety of other features such as URL previews that will show you what a link to one of your web pages looks like in the search engine results page (SERP).

How to Use Google Search Console for Your Business

Google Search Console offers a few different features that can be very beneficial for your company. Google Search Console allows you to register for free and add a domain to your website. It will then ask you to verify domain ownership. You will need to be able to access your domain service provider, where you purchased your domain.

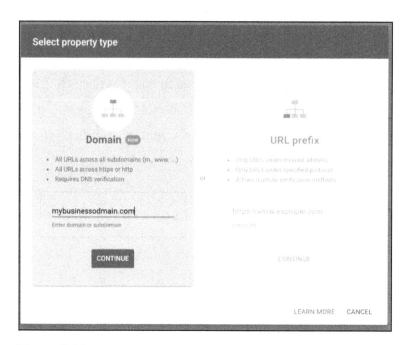

Figure 2.20

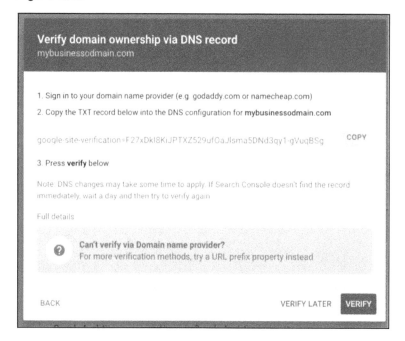

Figure 2.21

After verification is complete, you will have to wait up to 48 hours, but most likely you will see your Google sites on your domain in a few hours.

The URL Inspection tool can be used to request crawling once you have registered the site with verification. For detail, you can refer to Ask Google to recrawl your URLs(https://support.google.com/webmasters/answer/6065812).

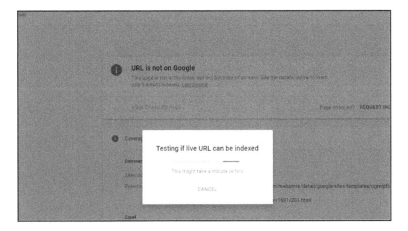

Figure 2.22

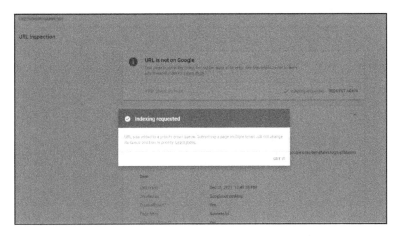

Figure 2.23

This is something that takes weeks to get indexed and then months to rank well compared to other websites, according to Google's Search Console Help Article.

For Google Workspace Admin

The following steps are for Google Workspace Admins who need to add a domain they own to their workspace.

Go to the Google Workspace Admin console, Custom URL page under 'Settings for Sites'.

https://docs.google.com/document/d/1HhhEfSAevusyle3C2OETXeGq_2UaoB7DYo d83nuEiKU/edit#

To add a custom URL, click the + icon

Figure 2.24

Click continue. The classic site can no longer be selected.

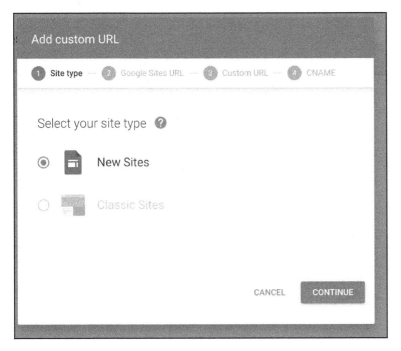

Figure 2.25

Enter your google sites URL. Please remove 'https://' and 'home' and click continue.
As an example, if your Google site URL is
https://sites.google.com/domain.com/event-testevent-test/home, enter
sites.google.com/domain.com/event-testevent-test

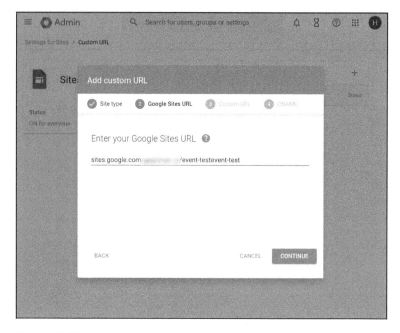

Figure 2.26

Select the domain you want to add to the site. Enter www instead of a subdomain name if you want the main domain.

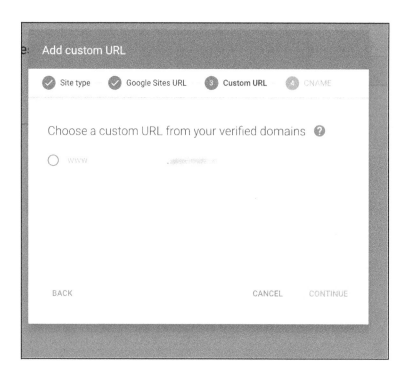

Figure 2.27

As you can see, you need to enter a cname. I used the subdomain ddd in this example.

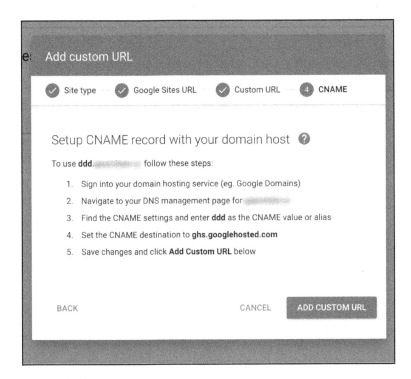

Figure 2.28

You will see the status change to complete once you have completed the above steps.

Figure 2.29

Please refer to the above Google search console guide for the remaining steps.

Three Ways to Transfer Ownership of Google Sites

Google Sites is a free and easy-to-use website builder that lets you create and share your website with the world. It's perfect for personal use, such as creating a portfolio site or organizing family photos, to professional use such as running a business. You can access Google Sites on the web or through their mobile app.

You might not know this, but Google Sites can be transferred in just a few clicks. Whether you're transferring to another person or company, the site will automatically update and give the new owner all of the permissions that you had when you first created it.

How to Transfer Ownership

You can transfer ownership of your site in three different ways:

Option 1. Add a user and invite them as an owner

The easiest way to transfer ownership of your site is by choosing the Transfer Ownership button in your Google Site settings. This will give whoever you want access to the same permissions that you had when you first created the site.

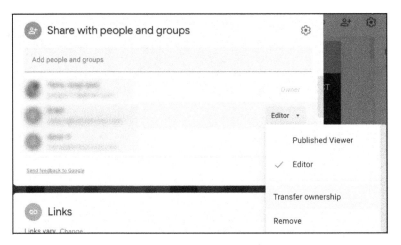

Figure 2.30

Click the 'Share with others' button at the top of the menu, add the email address of the person you want to transfer ownership to, and choose 'Transfer ownership' from the drop-down menu. Ownership request invitations will then be sent to that user, and ownership will be transferred upon acceptance.

However, if you are using Google Workspace (formerly G Suite), the new Google Sites does not allow you to transfer an owner to outside of your domain user. That brings us to the next method.

Option 2. Transfer via Google Shared Drives
Open Google Drive and search the website you wish to transfer ownership of (enter command type:site). And then drag and drop and move to a Shared Drive. This way, the site is no longer owned by an individual user. Now you can share to the outside domain user and manage the site with an editor (or editors).

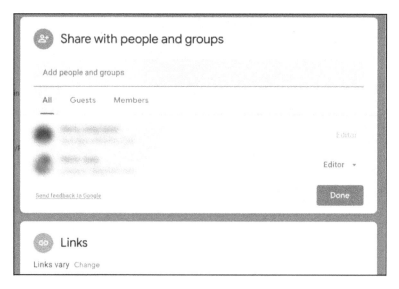

Figure 2.31

The problem in this method is that Shared Drives are only available on Google Workspace Business Standard or higher editions. Therefore, we are left with the next option as our last resort.

Option 3. Copy instead of transferring

If none of the above methods work, you can invite a user as a collaborator and have the user copy the site instead. As a result, the site can be copied under the new owner and wallah!

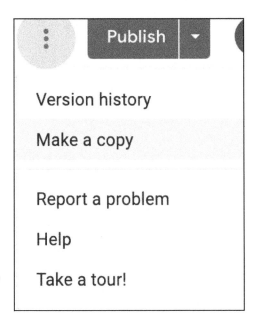

Figure 2.32

The best way to copy a set of Google Sites pages

Let's say you find yourself in a situation where you need to perform A/B testing on a particular page, to change the look and feel of the page or to copy the certain pages only. Instead of copying the entire site, you can begin by copying one or more pages.

Here's how. Click three vertical dots on the top right of the Google Sites edit mode, select 'Make a copy' menu option.

Figure 2.33

Enter the name of the new site and choose 'Selected page(s)' option. Click 'Next'.

Figure 2.34

Now you can select which pages you want to make a copy of.

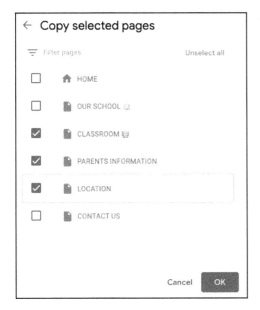

Figure 2.35

In addition, you can expand any pages with subpages to see them all. Click "Select All" to the right to select all subpages within a page, or select each page you would like to copy. You can see that only selected pages are copied in a newly created website.

Figure 2.36

CHAPTER 3 Mastering Google Sites

You are familiarizing yourself with Google Sites. It's time to take things to the next level. As you read this chapter, you will learn how to make the most of Google Sites, and you will see professional tips, know-hows, and examples.

How to Create a Custom Google Sites Theme

There are some Google Sites themes that have limited customization options. While you can tweak them to change the colors and fonts, there are certain elements that are pre-defined and cannot be modified.

A custom theme on Google Sites gives you more control over how your site looks and feels. Not only does it let you make small tweaks, but you can also go wild with it to completely personalize your site. I will explain what a Google Site theme is and how to create one of your own and manage them.

What Is a Google Site Theme?

A Google Site theme is a collection of formatting styles that are applied to your site's elements, such as banner, color scheme, font type.

You can create your own custom theme or use an existing one. Like a color palette or a mood board, Google Sites themes let you express yourself and your brand through design. A good site theme can attract and engage your target audience, make it easier to navigate your site, and help you achieve your marketing goals.

You can use themes to create consistent design elements across your site, or to create a completely customized design. Google's default themes are easy to modify and can be used as a base for creating a custom design.

How to Create a Custom Google Site Theme

The first step before you start creating your very own custom theme is to open a

Google Site and choose the "Themes" menu on the right pane. If you want to create a brand new custom theme, click the "+" button under the "Custom" option. If you want to use an existing theme as a starting point, choose a theme from "Created by Google".

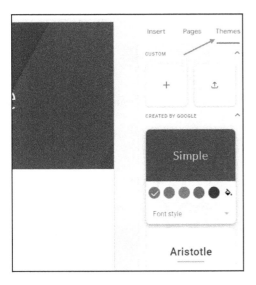

Figure 3.1

Create the Base of Your New Google Site Theme

Depending on what kind of custom theme you want to create, you can start with any Google Site theme as a base.

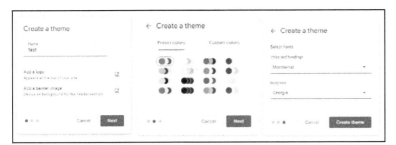

Figure 3.2

You can add a logo, a banner image for the homepage, choose color schemes and font styles. In the case of themes made by google, you can use their default theme or you can adjust it.

Import your Google Site Custom Theme

Importing a custom theme has the benefit that if you have another Google Sites project that needs to follow the identity of your company, you can simply import your custom theme instead of copying the existing website. It's true that you can just copy a previously made website but the problem is that you have to delete all the pages/contents, which causes cumbersome process steps.

With the custom theme import feature, you can import your design theme with the same look and feel without importing entire contents or pages.

To import your custom theme, click the import button under the "Custom" option. Then you can choose your custom theme from the popup menu.

Figure 3.3

After you import your custom theme, you will see a screen similar to the one below. Notice that you have your custom theme added under the "Theme" menu option.

Figure 3.4

Your Ultimate Guide to Creating CTA Custom Buttons for Google Sites

The buttons on your website are often the first impression that potential customers get of your business. Buttons may seem like a small detail, but they can make a big difference in the overall design and effectiveness of your site.

You need Call-To-Action, or CTA buttons to get your visitors to take certain actions to generate opportunities and sales. Make your Google Sites stand out by designing custom CTA buttons.

Google Sites offers three options for CTA buttons: Filled, Outline, and Text. However, if you want your site to be attractive and professional, you need to add more style. I'll show you how to create beautiful CTA buttons and icons for your Google Sites.

Option 1: Use Free Button Generator

There are many free button generators available on the internet if you search for them on Google.

For this demo, I have used 'Da button Factory'. Enter button text for CTA like 'Contact Sales' or 'Get Started', change font and button style, background, size, and color, and then download. The button can be embedded into your Google Sites once you download it. It's as simple as that.

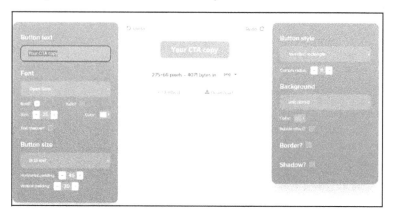

Figure 3.5

To resize a button in Google Sites, use the 'uncrop' option. It will automatically resize with the same ratio as the button.

Figure 3.6

Option 2: Use Google Drawing & Slides

However, if you want to further design buttons with background images or icons, you can use google drawings. Just go to Google Drive and create a new Google Drawings.

Upload images to embed within your icon, enter text for CTA and save as graphic images such as PNG, JPG format.

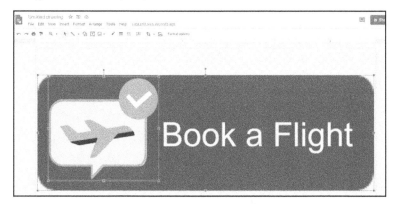

Figure 3.7

Again, you can adjust the button size using the 'uncrop' option. Add a hyperlink so that when users click the link, they go to your designated landing page.

Figure 3.8

Option 3: Hire Google Sites Designers

If you wish to make better and more professional buttons, icons, and banners but you don't have the time or resources, contact the professional designers for Google Sites. With color schemes and styles, they can align with your Brand Identity (BI), Corporate Identity (CI) with graphic tools like Adobe Photoshop or Illustrator.

Embed Content as a Full Page in Google Sites

Google Sites lets you add content as a full page. You can add custom code, another website, and Google apps like Google Maps, YouTube as fully functioning full pages.

Rather than showing the content within a page, this allows you to display the entire piece as a page. With this update, editors have more freedom to organize and display embedded content.

Site editors can add content from multiple sources including custom code, other websites, and Google apps, such as Maps and Docs.

To do so, go to 'Pages' and click the plus circle (+) on the lower right corner to add any content as a full page. Click 'Full page embed' <>

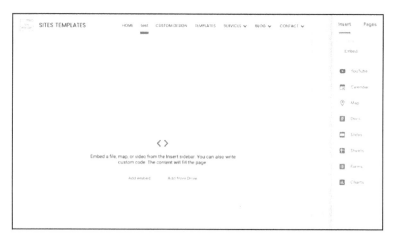

Figure 3.9

Notice 'Add embed', 'Add form Drive' and Google Apps under Insert menu options.

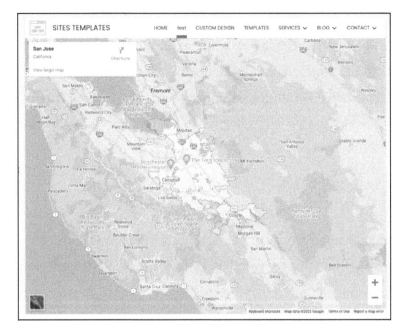

Figure 3.10

An example of embedding Google Maps as a full page.

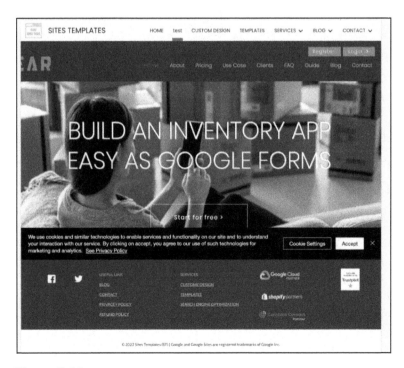

Figure 3.11

Yes! You can embed another entire website as a full page within your Google Site. Name the page and add a URL, embed code, 'Add from Drive' or embed content from another google apps such as Youtube, Calendar, Map, Docs, Slides, Sheets, Forms or Charts as well as Google Drive by clicking apps under the 'Insert' pane.

Embed a Clock and Countdown widgets for Google Sites

Today, everyone is online. A vast majority of people spend their time online on different websites. You may need to add useful widgets to differentiate your website and give it a personal touch.

The clock widget and countdown widget are two of the most common and useful widgets. With them, you can build an interactive website without much effort. I'll explain how to add clock and countdown widgets to your website in less than 10 minutes!

Add a Countdown Widget to Your Website and Drive Traffic

A countdown widget is a visual or textual countdown that tells website visitors when a particular event will occur. It's a great way to incorporate urgency into your marketing strategy and encourage your audience to take action right away. In most cases, businesses use countdown widgets to promote sales and special offers — but they can be used for many different types of campaigns! Countdown widgets also come in several different styles, which means you can choose the one that best aligns with your brand and marketing strategy.

This website (https://logwork.com/countdown-timer), for example, offers a free countdown widget and you can embed it on your Google Sites.

Figure 3.12

Customizing the widget style is pretty straightforward. Choose the Time for your future event, time zone, style, language, title of the countdown, style, text color etc.

And then click the [Embed on your website] button to get your script code like this. If you can read the code, you can edit from this script itself.

<script src="https://cdn.logwork.com/widget/countdown.js"></script>
<a href="https://logwork.com/countdown-7m5c" class="countdown-timer"
data-style="flip2" data-timezone="America/Los_Angeles" data-date="2022−12−25
00:00">Christmas Countdown</a>

Now you can just embed this code within your Google Sites like this.

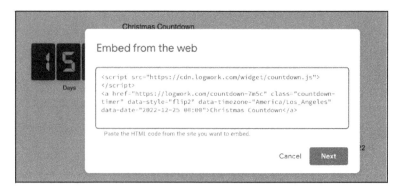

Figure 3.13

Add a Clock Widget to Your Website

Having a clock on your website is a great way to keep readers engaged and on your website for longer. What's more, adding a clock to your website can increase engagement by an incredible amount. A clock allows your customers to keep track of the time and know when it's best to finish their task at hand. This allows them to stay on your website while working. These days, it's common to see people on their phones while in the same room as friends and family. If you want to keep your readers on your website and engage with your content, a clock widget will help you do so.

Clock widgets are available on websites like (https://logwork.com/clock-widget-digital) and other (https://www.timeanddate.com/clocks/free.html) websites. Here are the examples and codes.

Figure 3.14

<script src="https://cdn.logwork.com/widget/digital.js"></script>
<a href="https://logwork.com/current-time-in-santa-clara-united-states-utah"
class="digital-clock" data-style="round" data-size="400"
data-timezone="America/Los_Angeles" data-language="en">Current time in Santa
Clara, United States</a>

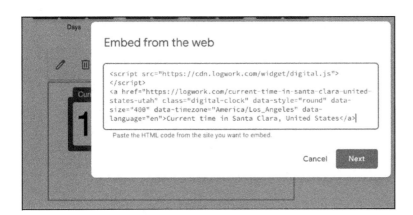

Figure 3.15

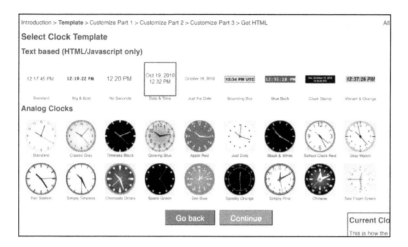

Figure 3.16

<iframe

src="https://free.timeanddate.com/clock/i8f95wfi/n283/tt0/tw0/tm1/ts1/tb4"

frameborder="0" width="87" height="34"></iframe>

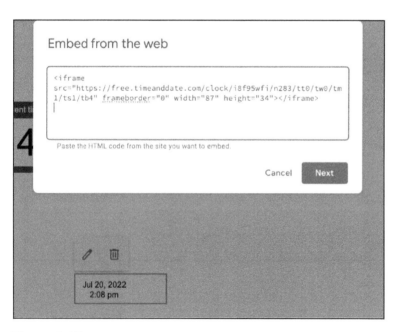

Figure 3.17

Sample websites with embedded clocks and countdown widgets can be found

here. (https://sites.google.com/view/clock12345/home).

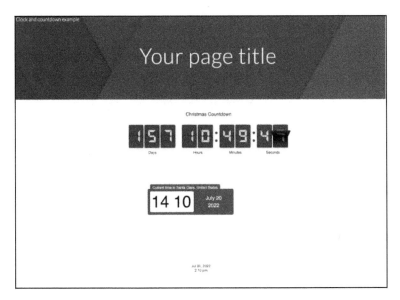

Figure 3.18

Adding Google My Business Review Widgets to My Google Sites

Adding a Google My Business (or GMB) Review Widget to your Google Sites can significantly increase trust and engagement with your potential customers. It may seem like a small addition, but its impact can be substantial. So, follow these steps, and let your happy customers do the talking for you.

Please note that Google does not provide a native tool for embedding Google Reviews in Google Sites. However, there are workarounds and alternative ways to add widgets to your Google Sites.

What is Google Review?

Google Reviews is a feature that allows users to write reviews for places they've visited, experiences they've had, and services they've received, among other things. These reviews are then publicly available on Google for others to read. You can find Google Reviews on Google Maps listing.

How can you increase Google Review?

Did you know that you can easily ask your customer to leave a review on your google maps? Using the Place ID finder(https://developers.google.com/maps/documentation/places/web-service/place-id#find-id), you can find your business listing review link.

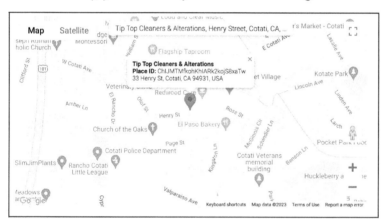

Now that you know the Place ID, you can add place ID identifier on this link

https://search.google.com/local/writereview?placeid=yourPlaceID
https://search.google.com/local/writereview?placeid=ChIJMTMfkohKhIARk2kojS8xaTw

Next, create a button on your Google Site like [Leave a Review] and add the above link, so that your client can leave a five star review on your business.

Also, you can get the 'See all review' link from google search. Search your business on google and notice the google map info on the right side pane. Find 'View all Google reviews' link and just copy the link, create a button and link to it.

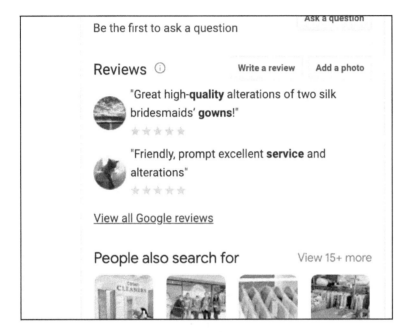

Add Google Review Widget

You can easily add Google Review to your website. Go to your business on Google Maps, click the reviews tab and click the share button to get the URL of the review.

And then just copy this link to your google sites with 'Embed' option.

You can click the 'Gear' icon and change options to show or hide image, title or description. Eventually, you can have something like this.

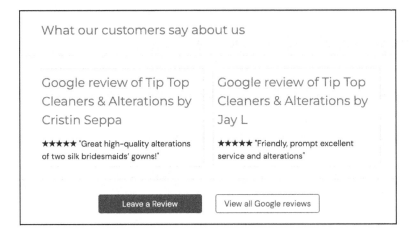

Side Note: Third Party Google Review Widget Worth it?

There are tons of third party Google Review widgets available, the most benefit is that it gives you the dynamic carousel style feed that you can browse and update with the latest reviews. But the downside is that most of them come with paid subscription or free with their brand badge.

How to Build a Discussion Forum to Your Google Sites

Conversations about your content can be a great way to get feedback. A discussion forum can provide a space for readers to talk with one another and involve more people in the discussion. Adding a discussion forum to your Google Sites site is easy. Here's how to do it.

What is a discussion forum?

The purpose of a discussion forum is to stimulate and promote public discourse about the content or topic. The tone varies depending on the community, but will generally be informal enough for people from all walks of life to participate in discussions with each other.

What are the benefits of adding a discussion to my site?

One of the benefits of adding a forum to your site is a chance for meaningful engagement with readers. You can create questions that are open-ended and allow for discussion, like "What are your thoughts on this article?"

You'll also have opportunities to hear from more people about your content — not just those who comment or email you. The more perspectives you can gather, the better you will be able to produce quality content.

Moreover, Google has seen a significant increase in ad impressions thanks to discussions. With these forums, advertisers are able to offer discounts and coupons as well as answer any questions that pop up in the discussion section. This can lead to increased conversions and sales if you have an e-commerce store.

How do I create a discussion on my site?

Google Groups(https://groups.google.com/my-groups) is a great way to get started in creating discussion forums on your website. After making the group public and allowing external users to view conversations, you can embed it into Google Sites and use it as a forum like our Discussion Forum page (https://sites.google.com/site/sitestemplate11/forum). Anyone can join the discussion and post. On the other hand, if your discussion forum has to be for internal use only, you can do so by adjusting the group access settings.

Figure 3.19

You can select the style of your logo, preview, edit, share, or buy your logo once you select your options.

Setting Up an ECommerce Store on Google Sites

Creating an e-commerce store on Google Sites can be a cost-effective and straightforward solution for individuals and small businesses looking to start selling products online. Google Sites, a free website builder from Google, offers an intuitive interface and easy integration with payment service tools, making it an attractive option for those already using Google's ecosystem. In this guide, we'll walk you through the process of setting up your ecommerce store on Google Sites.

Step 1. Sign in to Google Sites and Create a New Site

Go to sites.google.com and log in with your Google account. If you don't have one, create a new Gmail account for free. Select a template that suits your ecommerce store's style or start as blank. You can always customize the template later. Or, you can buy the premium google sites template from sitestemplates.net.

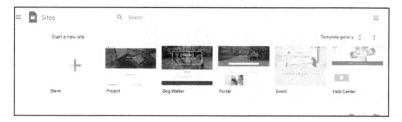

Step 2. Design Your ECommerce Store

Plan your site's structure by creating essential pages like "Home," "Shop," "About Us," "Contact," and "FAQ." You can add more pages as needed. Organize your site's navigation menu by clicking on "Pages" in the sidebar. Drag and drop pages to arrange them in the desired order. Ensure that the design aligns with your brand identity and provides a user-friendly experience for visitors.

Step 3. Set Up Payment and Checkout Options

Research and choose a suitable payment gateway for your e-commerce store. Popular options include Stripe and PayPal, as both are free services, so I'll include them in this article.

Option 1: Paypal

PayPal stands out as one of the most well-known payment gateways, offering easy creation of a "Buy Now" button.

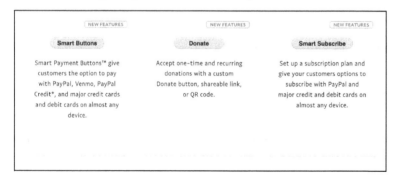

Pros: With just a few clicks, you can generate a "Buy Now" button and use Smart buttons or Smart Subscribe buttons to set up one-time or recurring payments.

Embedding the code into Google Sites is a breeze. Check out this start page for more details: https://www.paypal.com/buttons/

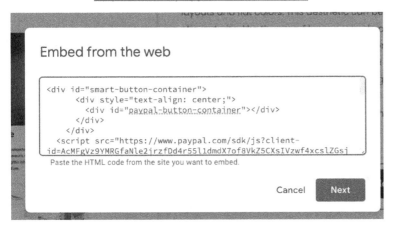

Cons: However, it lacks advanced features like bulk item management, coupons, and an advanced checkout system to handle multiple items.

Option 2: Stripe

Stripe is a highly popular payment gateway service, offering a wide range of features. Let's explore its pros and cons.

Pros: One of its main advantages is the extensive array of features, including efficient management of multiple products and the ability to create promotional campaign coupons.

Cons: Nevertheless, its biggest drawback is the variety of fees it charges. Even in cases where you have to issue refunds due to customer purchase mistakes, you still end up paying fees. Additionally, their current pricing table widget does not function well on Google Sites.

Step 4. Add Your Products

Create a new page for your online store or modify the existing "Shop" page. Add your products with relevant details such as product names, descriptions, prices, and images. Organize them into categories for easy navigation. Add the necessary payment buttons or widgets to your product pages to enable secure and convenient transactions.

Four Options to Add Live Chat to Your Google Sites

Live chat is one of the most effective ways to provide customer service, build customer loyalty and drive website conversions. This feature allows businesses to interact with customers in real-time, providing an engaging, personalized experience that can boost customer satisfaction and loyalty. Not only does live chat provide customers with an immediate response to their questions, but it also offers businesses a variety of benefits, such as increased sales, improved customer service, and greater customer engagement.

By integrating a live chat feature into your Google Sites, businesses can take advantage of these benefits and create a better customer experience. Here are four types of live chats that you can implement to your Google Sites.

Option 1: Live Chat widget with expanding floating screen.

Almost all live chat widgets, including Tidio, Elfsight, Testmator are expanding embedded chat. Visitors can chat with an agent upon clicking the chat button and can have a conversation within the expandable floating screen.

However, Google Sites does not support dynamic live chats like this. When a user clicks the chat button, the expanded screen does not float, but remains stuck within the code area. As an example, instead of showing this, you'll see this screen.

You expected this:

Figure 3.20

In reality, Google Sites work like this:

Figure 3.21

In order to show an expanded area, you need to ensure that there is enough code area so that when the user clicks a button, it expands and becomes visible within the code area.

Pros & Cons:

- Pros: The screen is expandable and interactive. It is ideal for any website.
- Cons: Google Sites does not support expandable live chats. The workaround is to have more space for the entire code area, taking into account the expandable screen.

Option 2: Expanded Live Chat

You can embed already expanded live chat instead of expanding live chat on Google Sites. So, your visitors will be able to communicate in a comprehensive chat room.

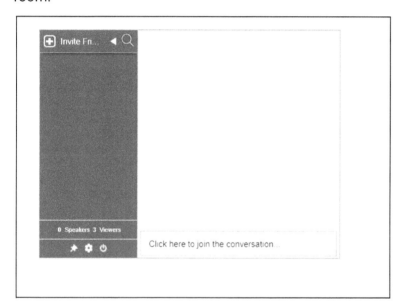

Figure 3.22

Pros & Cons:

- Pros: The chat window is comprehensive.
- Cons: Chat area occupies too much space.

Option 3: Button Image to Live Chat

It is also possible to create a chat button with a hyperlink so that the user can start a conversation in a different tab or page. It's not as convenient or fancy as the first option, but it works well for Google sites. When your website visitor sees that your agent is online, he or she clicks to contact an agent.

Figure 3.23

Pros & Cons:
- Pros: A simple solution for Google Sites. Upon clicking a button, the user will be taken to the next screen where the conversation will begin.
- Cons: The appearance is not outstanding, and the user cannot continue their conversation on the same screen.

Option 4: WhatsApp as Live Chat

The final but not the last option is to use social media gadgets such as WhatsApp. The Whatsapp website widget is simple and easy to use. It is possible to utilize your WhatsApp phone number for online conversations, and when a visitor presses the live chat button, the message is then dispersed through WhatsApp. Moreover, these live chat widget services are offered at no cost, though the features are somewhat restricted.

Figure 3.24

For example, you can simply put this code on your website. Replace phone number to yours with country code. For example, the phone number on this code is +1−408−555−5555

```
<a href="https://api.whatsapp.com/send?phone=14085555555" style="display: inline-block; padding:16px; border-radius: 8px; background-color: #25D366; color: #fff; text-decoration: none; font-family: sans-serif; font-size: 16px;">Contact us on WhatsApp</a>
```

Pros & Cons:

- Pros: Embed your existing social app and start a conversation with your visitors without having to worry about paid plans.
- Cons: The visitor would need the same social media app as Whatsapp.

Your Live chat choice

If you decide to integrate a live chat feature on your Google Sites and use a third-party application, you'll have to select the right application to meet your needs. The most important thing to know before picking a live chat application is what each type does and how it's compatible. With live chat on your Google site, your interaction with visitors will improve and your chances of winning sales will increase.

How to Build Multi-Language Google Sites and Connect with Subdomains

A Google Sites is very easy to design, so if you want additional language on your site, you can simply copy the entire site and translate it with different languages. You'll need a custom domain once you've translated your site.

Here's how you can add an additional domain to your Google Domains account for your 2nd language Google site.

Suppose you already have yourbusiness.com as your main landing page, but you want to have ko.yourbusiness.com for the Korean version.

As a first step, please add a custom domain ko.yourbusiness.com to your Google Sites settings. Note that only the owner of google sites can add a domain under settings.

Next thing is logging into your Google Domains account, selecting the domain name and going to the 'Website' page to add a subdomain. Click on 'Build another website'

Figure 3.25

And then, click 'Continue' on the Simple site tile on this page.

Figure 3.26

Next — Choose 'Use existing site' since you already have one with Korean language.

Figure 3.27

Choosing your subdomain is the next step. I have put ko and selected already made Korean Google sites. Make sure you own the translated Google site. To prevent your main domain from being routed to the translated site, ensure that the option 'Also redirect....' is ticked off.

Figure 3.28

Click 'No, keep existing records' on this page. This popup may not disappear after clicking this, as it seems to be a glitch. Go back to the 'Website' page on your Google Domains once you have completed this step.

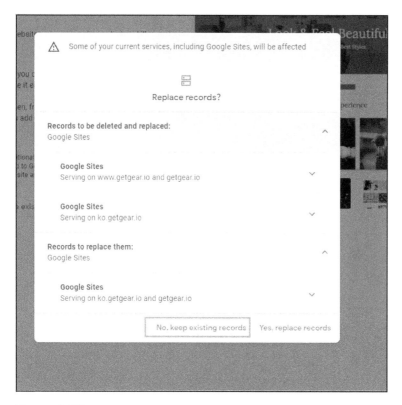

Figure 3.29

Now as you can see, subdomains are connected to translated websites.

Figure 3.30

Additionally, you will see that both English and Korean websites have DNS setup.

Figure 3.31

That's it! Oh, don't forget to link each other within Google Sites so users can select to visit their language site.

How to Build a Contact Us Form for Your Website That Generates Leads

Creating a contact us form on your website may not seem like the most exciting thing to do. But trust us, it's worth your while. Creating a contact form is one of the most effective ways of generating leads for your business. The more effective you are at getting visitors to fill out your contact form and click on the submission button, the more leads you will get from your website. After all, if people can't get in touch with you, they won't be able to buy anything from you!

What is a Contact Us Form?

Contact us forms are an essential part of any business website. They are a simple and easy way to receive customer inquiries via your website. A contact us form can be used to gather information about your business and products, as well as for potential clients to get in touch with you. Contact us forms are commonly found at the bottom of a website homepage or on separate pages dedicated for contact information (such as "Contact Us" or "Customer Service").

How to build a contact us form that generates leads?

There are a few things you'll need to do to build a contact us form that generates leads:

1. Identify the purpose of the form:

    You could use it to collect information about your products and services, or to collect email addresses.

2. Create a dedicated page:

    Make sure your contact form is on a separate page from the rest of your website so that it does not distract your visitors from what they came to see.

3. Write a compelling call to action (CTA):

    The visitor sees this content when they visit your website. It might say, 'Learn more about our products,' or 'Get in touch with us today.' Make sure your call to action is clear and to the point.

4. Include a brief explanation of how the contact us form works:

    Make sure your visitors understand how to utilize the form and where to send the information. Do not inundate them with too much data.

5. Keep it simple:

    You want visitors to be able to easily and quickly fill out the form. If they become confused, they will not finish the form and you will not be able to acquire their data.

Lead generation tools to assist with your Contact Us Form

Google Form

Google Forms is a free web-based survey app that is included as part of Google Docs. Using Google Forms, you can make a simple contact form that links to Google Sheets. Each time someone submits a form, it is automatically recorded to your linked Google Sheets. Forms can be customized by embedding your company logo, background image, or color theme.

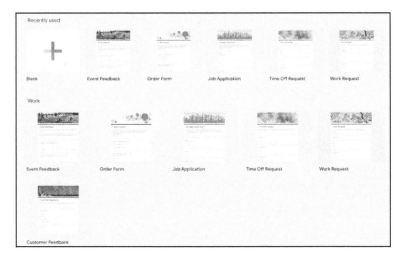

Figure 3.32

Jotform

Jotform is a popular and robust web application that provides templates for contact forms, store forms, payment forms, and more. The app is freemium, so you can use it for free and upgrade for advanced features or submission limits. The user can also add payment and check out options, a Google calendar, zoom functionality, and more.

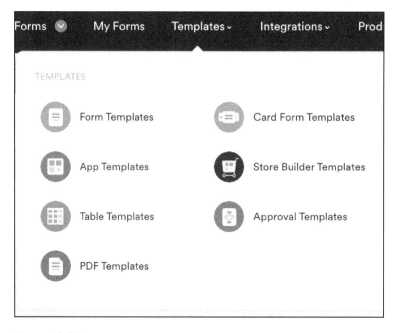

Figure 3.33

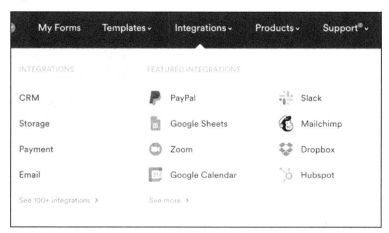

Figure 3.34

Jotform and Google Form can both be embedded into Google Sites easily. Take advantage of Google Sites and make your Google Sites that generate leads and opportunities.

SEO Tips for Google Sites

Google Sites is always Google's best choice to use electricity for web hosting. And, as always, Google offers a lot of advice and support to help people use its platforms and tools.

However, this is not the only resource you have when looking for the SEO mind map for your Google Sites. I have compiled this guide to help you get the information you need to develop your search engine optimization strategy.

What is SEO for Google Sites?

SEO for Google Sites is the process of optimizing Google Sites to improve their search engine rankings for relevant keywords. A good Google Sites SEO plan focuses on the essential HTML elements that search engines use to index and rank content in the SERPs.

Like any other type of website, Google sites are built with a Content Management System (CMS) such as WordPress and Wix, which can be optimized for SEO and ranked in the SERPs for relevant information.

When it comes to SEO, there are many best practices that you can use. After all, people in SEO have complete jobs! SEO is about using the right keywords and providing relevant information to your customers on your website. Here are some SEO tips for Google sites to help you get started:

Tip 1: Publish Relevant, Authoritative Content

      Quality, authoritative content is the number one factor for your search engine results, and nothing replaces the best content — this is especially true regarding SEO marketing. Good content created specifically for your target audience increases online traffic, which increases your site's authority and relevance. Improve your writing skills online and show yourself as an authority on the topic you are writing about.

Define and target a specific keyword for each legal page on your website. Consider how your reader will find that page with search information. It is challenging for a web page to achieve search engine ranking for many key phrases unless those phrases are similar. If you want to rank for multiple keywords on your website, you need to create a separate web page for each keyword you are targeting.

Besides the page URL, title, and subtitles, the most important factors are the search results. Repeat the keyword multiple times on the page — once or twice in the opening and closing paragraphs and two to four times in the rest of the content. Be in charge — links to relevant resources and additional information on your organization's public website and other useful websites.

Tip 2: Submit an XML Sitemap to Google

An XML sitemap acts as a template for your website. When search engines get this plan, they can analyze and rank more accurate content (crawling and indexing). Indexing is important because it determines which categories and search terms your content will appear on the results pages.

You can submit an XML map to Google Search Console (formerly Google Webmaster Tools) so that crawlers can access it for information. Here you can also check your position in the index and see areas for improvement.

Figure 3.35

However, If you are using Google Sites, you don't even need to submit XML since your Google Sites is already being indexed with built-in Google Search.

Tip 3: Optimize Page Speed & Get Rid of Bloat

Page speed is essential for performance, and Google will be the first to tell you. They also have tools to help you test your page speed and find areas that need improvement. Make sure you upload your images, put them in the most miniature format possible, and remove any extras you don't need. Skip ads and pop-ups and make sure there are no distractions. These days, you will lose points if you have too many pop-ups.

Page speed is all about giving people quick and easy answers. Simplify navigation and take advantage of mobile design to create a powerful site that is mobile-friendly and easy to load on any platform. You can use Google Analytics tools or find many other tools to test your page speed and identify areas for improvement.

Tip 4: Change Google Sites Permissions

The next step in SEO for Google Sites is to change the permission for the website to be published on the website. This allows people to search and open the site and gives Google crawlers access to the content. If you do not change this permission, your Google sites will not be indexed by Google, Yahoo, or Bing search engine.

To make your Google Site publicly available, click on the "Share with Others" icon at the top of the Site builder screen and then change the "Published Site" setting to make the website public. This setting change will allow your site to be crawled, indexed, and ranked in SERPs.

Tip 5: Get a Complimentary Google Sites SEO Audit

Anyone with a Google account can create their website free with Google Sites. Although this CMS platform is simpler and more limited than many competitors, it welcomes users and achieves its purpose of allowing users to publish quickly and easily. Combining a CMS with a Google Sites SEO plan means increasing your site's chances of ranking well, increasing traffic, and using your stuff.

There are benefits to any website when it comes to using Google Analytics, but if you're on Google Sites, it's a must. Not only will it tell you how your site is doing in traffic and rankings, but it will also tell you where your SEO efforts are working, maybe missing a sign and more. You can create different customizable reports to help you learn more about your SEO campaigns and what can be customized or optimized.

Takeaway

These five SEO tips and best practices are crucial steps you can take to improve your website. You make changes that will help customers and searchers better understand your business. However, sometimes people recommend SEO methods that do not bring success to visitors to the website and are only there to try to manage searches.

As you can see, Google Sites SEO is the process of improving Google sites to help them rank higher in search engine results pages (SERPs) for relevant information. And like other popular CMS platforms like Wix and WordPress, some HTML elements on Google Sites can also be optimized for SEO to increase your search engine rankings.

H1 and H2 Tags for Google Sites?

The H1 tag is used to provide a clear and concise heading for the main content of a webpage. This helps both users and search engines understand the main topic of the page, making it easier to navigate and more likely to rank well in search results.

Figure 3.36

```
="">Title-</span><span class="afVDVd C9DxTc " style:
O GORGEOUS</span></h1><h1 id="h.3vdfzw7t8iuo" dir="
-bottom: none; border-left: none; border-right: none
ight: 45.0pt; margin-top: 0.0pt; padding-bottom: 0.0
s="C9DxTc " style="">NEW COLLECTION</span></h1></div
 class="hJDwNd-AhqUyc-Clt0zb Ft7HRd-AhqUyc-Clt0zb j
 mGzaTb Depvyb baZpAe"><h3 id="h.2378fyum2d2h" dir='
.0pt; margin-right: 45.0pt; padding-left: 0.0pt; te:
```

Figure 3.37

It is generally recommended to use one H1 tag per page to ensure that the main topic is clear and concise. However, in Google Sites, there is no tag specifically labeled as H1. Instead, there are various text styles available, including normal text, title, heading, subheading, and small text.

When it comes to H2 tags — while there is no specific limit on the number of H2 tags that can be used on a page, it's generally recommended to use them sparingly and strategically. Too many H2 tags can make a page appear cluttered and difficult to read, which can negatively impact the user experience and potentially hurt the page's SEO

Normal text is represented by the <p> tag, while the title is represented by the H1 tag. The heading, subheading, and small text are represented by the H2, H3, and <small> tags, respectively.

In nutshell:

- Normal text: <p> tag
- Title: <H1> tag
- Heading: <H2> tag
- Subheading: <H3> tag
- smalltext: <small> tag

While it may be confusing to use a different labeling system for heading tags in Google Sites, it is still important to ensure that the main topic of each page is clearly identified using the appropriate heading tag. This will help both users and search engines understand the content of the page and improve the likelihood of ranking well in search results.

Why Adding Alt Tag Is Important When Optimizing Your Website For Search Engines

Search engines like Google, Bing, and Yahoo! use algorithms to determine which websites are worthy of being listed in their search results. These algorithms work by looking at multiple factors, including how relevant your website is to the search query, how many pages you have on your site, how unique your content is, and how many backlinks to other sites you have.

These algorithms are pretty complex, and even the best SEOs in the world can't really predict how the rankings of websites will change from one day to the next.

On top of that, the algorithms are constantly being updated and improved, making it even more difficult to keep up. So, how can you optimize your website to ensure that it ranks well in search engines? Well, the answer is simple: by adding alt tags to images on your site.

What are alt tags?

Alt tag is short for alternative text, which is just a plain, simple sentence that describes what the image is and what it's about.

Why are alt tags important?

Alt tags are important because they can help your website rank better in search engines. People now often conduct image searches as well. The key to getting good rankings is having an abundance of quality content about a specific topic. Search engines use this content to determine how relevant your website is to the search query typed into Google, Yahoo!, Bing, or any other engine.

For example, if you have a page on your site about dog breeds, you would want to upload images of different breeds and alt tag them with keywords related to the page like "dog breeds." If you don't have an image for a specific keyword, it's ok! You can also include text in your alt tag that describes the image. This makes it possible for people looking for something like "dog breeds" to find your website, no matter whether they had typed "dog breeds" or "french bulldog," both of which might be popular queries at any given time.

If you want to rank highly for a search term, be sure that all of the images on your website have descriptive alt tags. In order for an image to be relevant and useful in a search engine's ranking algorithm, it needs to have a brief but complete description of what's in the picture.

How to add alt tags to images on your website

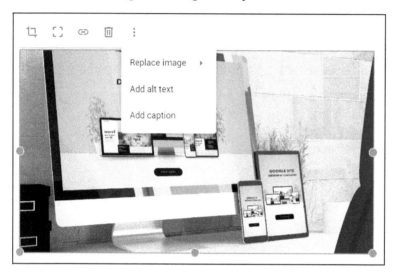

Figure 3.38

To enter an alt tag description in Google Sites, click the image in Google Sites, choose three dots, and select 'Add alt text'. And then enter the text for the image.

10 Must Have Components for Intranet Google Sites

Intranet Google Sites is an internal website for use within an organization. Intranet Google Sites are often used by large organizations to provide employees with a single point of contact for everything the company has to offer.

An intranet is different from a regular website because it's only accessible to your employees. An intranet isn't as general in nature as a website and contains information specific to your organization.

Intranet Google Sites provide a centralized access point for all types of organizational information, including organizational policies and procedures, employee directory, training schedules, and much more. One of the best ways to create an effective intranet is to have a set of components that you know will be useful for your employees.

1. Google Apps Service Menu Bar

Lots of companies that need an Intranet with Google Sites use Google Workspace to do their work. Having access to all the Google Apps services including Gmail, Drive, and Calendar on one page simplifies access for staff members.

Figure 3.39

2. Knowledge Base

One of the most important components for an intranet is a knowledge base. A knowledge base provides FAQs and educational information about your company's offerings. This is a great place for employees to get answers to common questions about your company, products and services. Also, common things like how to access WIFI, use network printers, how to set up an email on mobile phones- these are all good examples of articles for knowledge-base pages.

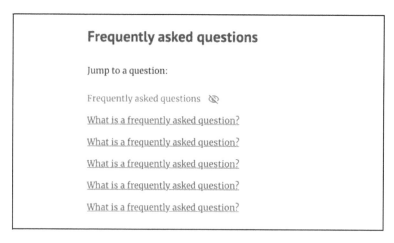

Figure 3.40

3. Discussion Forum

Intranet discussion forums provide a major boost for project management and company culture. Employees who feel like they can communicate openly and collaborate on projects often come up with innovations.

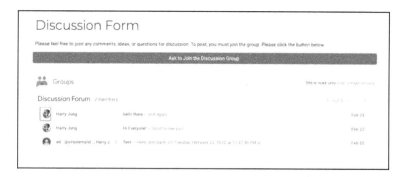

Figure 3.41

4. Events Calendar

Event calendar is a place where you can see or list upcoming events, such as company holidays, special events, training sessions and more. Events on this calendar could be in the form of a Google Calendar, a link to a website, or even just a date and time if you'd like. You can also use this space to provide details about the event along with any important information such as location, topic, or guest speakers.

Figure 3.42

5. Staff Directory

A staff directory is a place where you can list the various departments or teams within your organization and their contact information. It makes it easy for employees to find the right person to talk to when they need assistance. Employees can search for a specific department or individual using keywords, titles, or other terms.

Figure 3.43

6. Blog & News

Blogs are a great way to communicate with your team. They can be used to share company updates and provide helpful insights. Blogs are also an excellent way to encourage your team members to contribute content and get them involved in the intranet. Additionally, your intranet staff will benefit from important news around the company or industry.

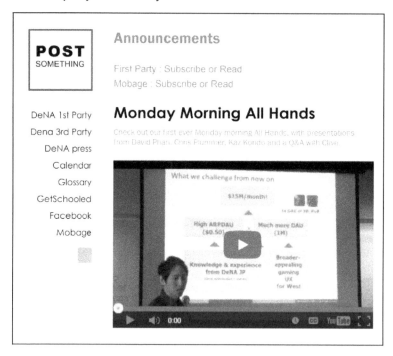

Figure 3.44

7. Projects Pages

A project page is a specific area on your intranet to list all of your current projects. From this page, team members can search for a specific project, view the team member working on it, and see the status.

Figure 3.45

8. Resources Library

A resource library is a place where your team members can access and see the shared information. A good resource library will include templates for documents and presentations, as well as links to helpful resources. You can also use the resource library to store information about policies or other important company-wide information. Resources should be carefully curated, so that you can provide the best possible tools for your team to work smarter.

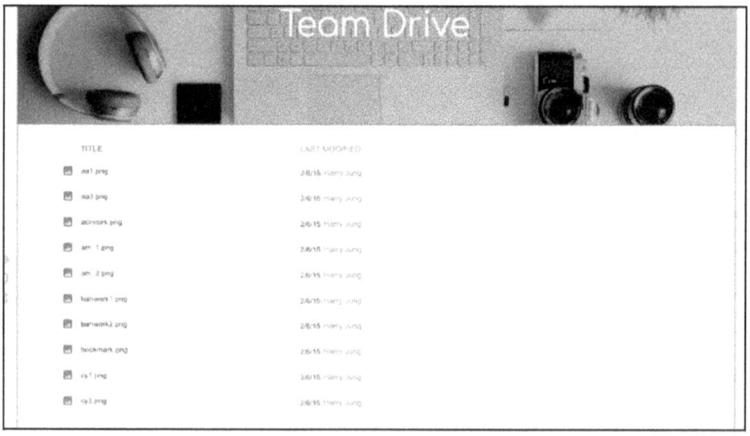

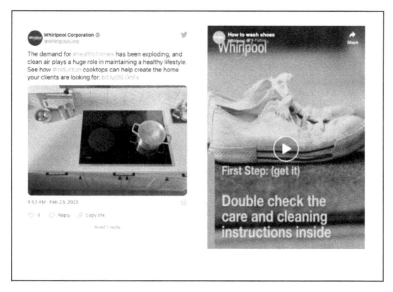

Figure 3.46

9. Social Media Integration

If you're looking to build a stronger connection between your team, it might be worth including social media integration in your intranet. A lot of companies rely on social media sites like Twitter and Facebook to communicate with their team. If this is the case for you, then it's a good idea to make those tools available on your intranet as well.

Figure 3.47

10. Office Locations

If you have a location for your project sites or company, you can embed the Google Maps app to easily navigate them.

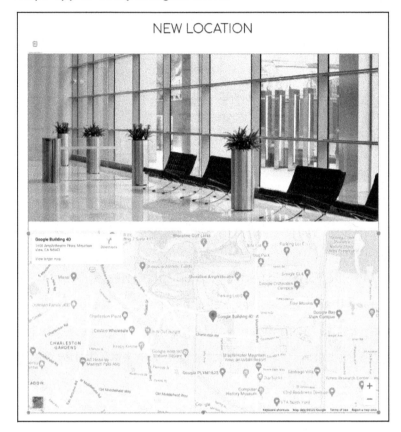

Figure 3.48

Intranets are a powerful tool for improving employee collaboration and knowledge sharing. By including these 10 Google Sites components for your intranet, your team can stay on top of projects and collaborate more effectively.

How to Create an Effective Landing Page Using Google Sites

Google Sites can be used for creating landing pages. With its customizable templates and drag-and-drop interface, it's a user-friendly solution for creating landing pages with a professional look and feel.

Benefits of Creating a Landing Page

There are many benefits of having a landing page. Here are some of the major benefits:

- Capture Leads: Landing pages are designed to attract targeted traffic and direct them towards one goal. Therefore, the main purpose of creating a landing page is to capture leads by encouraging targeted web visitors to sign up for your email list.
- Drive Traffic to Your Site: Landing pages also drive targeted traffic to your website. This means that if someone takes the desired action on your landing page, they will be redirected to your site. This is a good way to direct more traffic to your site, as your landing page will likely have higher organic search results than your homepage.
- Build Your Brand: Creating a landing page can also help you build your brand. When you create a landing page, you can incorporate your logo, brand colors, and other branding elements to help you build your brand online.
- Improve Your Conversion Rate: Finally, creating a landing page can help you improve your conversion rate. A well-designed landing page is focused on one goal, such as a sale or lead generation. By directing your focus to one goal, you can avoid distractions that might reduce your conversion rate.

Figure 3.49

What makes the perfect landing page?

When it comes to creating a high-converting landing page, there are several elements that you need to keep in mind both in marketing and technical. They are:

- Headline: Your headline is the first thing that people will see when they come to your landing page. You need to create a headline that immediately captures the attention of your target audience. Additionally, your headline should be aligned with your target audience.
- Offer Button with Call-To-Action(CTA): The offer is what you're giving away on your landing page. It can be a free trial of your product, a discount on a product, or lead magnet. Make sure it stands out from the rest of your text, and make sure it's easy to click.
- Graphics: Visual content is extremely important when it comes to marketing in landing pages. A well-designed image or image collage can help you

increase your conversion rate. Make sure to use high-quality images that help illustrate your value proposition and add visual appeal to your page.

- Concise and persuasive copy: The copy on your landing page is just as important as the other elements. The text on your landing page needs to be short and descriptive. Use clear and persuasive copy to explain why your offering is the best solution for your target audience's needs.

Optimizing Your Landing Page for Conversions

Once you have designed your landing pages in Google Sites, you should check and improve these factors.

- Mobile responsiveness: Ensure your landing page is optimized for mobile devices and provides a seamless experience for users on any device. Luckily, google sites are mobile responsive and you don't need to worry about building a separate webpage for mobile or tablet devices.
- A/B testing: Once you've created a landing page in Google Sites, you can continuously test and optimize your page for performance by creating a new version for A/B testing. This will help you discover what changes need to be made to improve your conversion rate. You can easily make a copy of Google Sites and build another version with a different look and feel.
- Load speed: Optimize your landing page for fast load speed to reduce bounce rates and increase conversions. Test your website's loading speed with a free website speed test and optimize your images to make them load faster.

Embed CSS on Google Sites: Text Box

Google Sites is your gateway to ultimate customization. With the ability to apply script and CSS, as well as choose from a wide range of Google fonts, your site will be a unique masterpiece.

And if you're looking to add some creative flair to your text, there are a few tricks up our sleeve. Use the code font for a simple, yet effective way to display text within a box with a background color. Or, if you want to take it a step further, add some CSS code to create rounded rectangles with custom fonts and background images or colors.

Use Code Font

If you're looking to place your text within a box with a background color, the 'Code Font' is the simplest solution. You can easily select the code font and then customize it with the font of your choice.

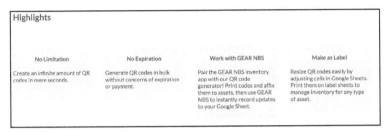

Figure 3.50

Here's how:

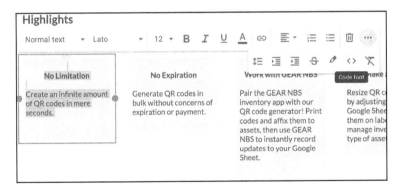

Figure 3.51

Embed CSS for Beautification

Another option is to include CSS code directly on your Google Site. This can allow you to place text within rounded rectangles with custom background images or colors. You can also select from a variety of Google fonts to further personalize your site.

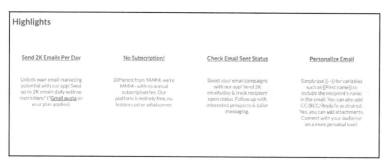

Figure 3.52

Here's how:

Figure 3.53

Here's the sample code:

```
<link href="https://fonts.googleapis.com/css?family=Lato&display=swap"
rel="stylesheet">
<style>
P{
Border-radius:20px;
Padding:20px;
Color:royalblue;
Background-color:efefef;
```

```
Font-size:14px;
font-family: 'Lato', cursive;
Text-align:center;
}
</style>
<p>
```

Unlock your email marketing potential with our app! Send up to 2K emails daily with no restrictions* (*<a href="https://support.google.com/a/answer/166852" target="_blank">Gmail quota</a> on your plan applies).

```
</p>
```

There you have it — the tools to create a stunning website!

CHAPTER 4 Go Beyond Google Sites

This chapter will cover a wide range of Google Sites use cases in different applications and platforms, going much beyond just Google Sites. You will see the full potential of Google Sites.

Convert Google Sites as an Unlimited Storage Space

In today's digital world, we have to manage and store a lot of files. Google Photos, for example, allows me to sync my iPhone photos to Google Photo storage. However, it's becoming more expensive to store my data as time goes by, because I have to buy more storage and pay a monthly fee.

Google sites can be used as a personal website, company website, or intranet. You can even use Google sites as a photo repository space.

Google sites do not use any storage space, unlike google docs or non-google docs files like PDFs. Yes! Google Sites can be used as storage, allowing you to back up all of your photos and consume no Google Drive storage. For example, you can upload your photos to Google Sites and keep them safe.

I'll show you how to do it. The first step is to create a Google Site. You can then make an album page and select photos on it. You can upload entire photos at once if you choose. No need to upload pictures one by one.

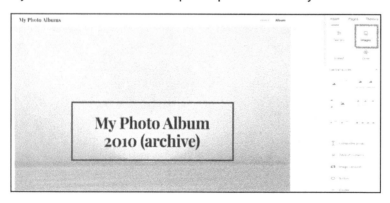

Figure 4.1

Select the 'Images' button and click on the photo images you want to upload to the page.

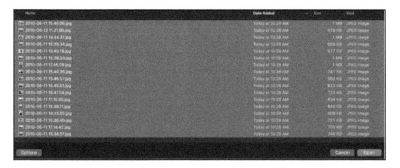

Figure 4.2

Your Google Site is now a photo album and backup location! You no longer have to worry about purchasing additional storage or anything like that.

Figure 4.3

Photos are uploaded to the page.

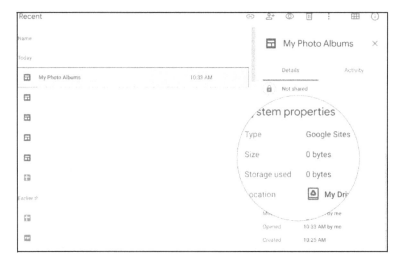

Figure 4.4

Notice that "ZERO" storage is used on your Google Drive.

Using Google Sites as a Stock Image Search Tool

Google Sites has a built-in image search function that allows you to find royalty-free images from a variety of sources. To use it, simply open Google Sites and click on the "Images" tab. Then, type in your keyword and hit enter.

Google Sites will then show you a list of images that match your keyword. You can click on any image to view it larger or to get more information about it.

The best part about using Google Sites as a stock image search tool is that you don't have to visit places like Adobe images, Shutterstock or Getty Images separately. Instead, you can find relevant images for your keyword right within Google Sites.

And, because Google Sites uses a variety of sources for its images, you're sure to find the perfect image for your needs. This means you can find images from hundreds of stock image providers.

In summary, there are several benefits to using Google Sites as a stock image search tool, including:

- It's quick and easy to use.
- You can find royalty-free images from a variety of sources.
- You don't have to visit places like Shutterstock or Getty Images separately.
- You can find relevant images for your keyword right within Google Sites.

How to use Google Sites as a stock image search tool

Figure 4.5

To use Google Sites as a stock image search tool, follow these steps:

1. Open Google Sites.
2. Click on the "Section colors" tab. Choose 'Image > Select'.
3. Select 'Search' and enter the keyword for the image that you are looking for and hit enter.
4. Google Sites will then show you a list of images that match your keyword.
5. Click on any image and notice that you can find the image source URLs and can visit the website as well.

🎉 Embracing Emojis: The New Google Sites Update and Why It Matters 🚀

Adding emojis to a website can offer several benefits, both from a user experience and a branding perspective. From expressing emotions to capturing attention, these tiny symbols have a big impact.

Figure 4.6

Why Emojis Matter for Your Website

1. Human Touch: Emojis can make your content feel more relatable, adding a human touch to your brand's online presence.

2. Attention Grabbers: Their vibrant nature can make your headlines pop, ensuring your content doesn't go unnoticed.

3. Universal Appeal: Emojis speak a global language, making them perfect for websites catering to an international audience.

4. Boost Engagement: Make your content more interactive and engaging with the right emoji.

5. Space Savers: Convey more with less! Emojis can summarize emotions and actions in a single symbol.

6. Enhance Brand Voice: Consistent use of emojis can make your brand instantly recognizable and memorable.

How to Use the Emoji Feature on Google Sites

1. Open Your Google Site: Navigate to the page you want to edit.

2. Access the Toolbar: Click on the toolbar where you typically find text editing options.

3. Search for Emojis: With the new update, you'll find an emoji search option. Simply type in the emotion or object you're looking for, and a range of emojis will appear.

4. Add to Your Site: Click on your desired emoji, and it will be added to your title, text bar, or even the navigation bar.

Figure 4.7

Figure 4.8

How to Use Google Sites as Bookmark Manager

The Internet is an endless source of information. If you're looking for something in particular, like how to build a bookshelf or the population of Uruguay, the chances are that you'll find what you're looking for with just a few searches. But what if you come across a website or blog post that you know you'd want to revisit? In these instances, bookmarking websites comes in handy.

Many web browsers such as Chrome and Brave allow you to bookmark pages and link them to your account. However, what if you have multiple accounts or machines and want to keep your bookmarks somewhere safe? You may find it difficult to locate them when you need them right away.

Google Sites can be a great bookmark manager if you want to save websites. You may save a website to your Google site, and all you need to remember is your Google Sites URL; you don't even need to remember the URL, since Google sites are stored in your Google Drive and don't consume any storage space.

Create a blank Google Sites and go to the 'Pages' tab.

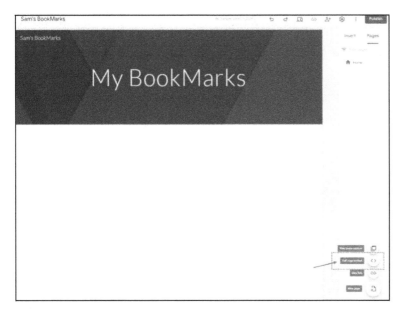

Figure 4.9

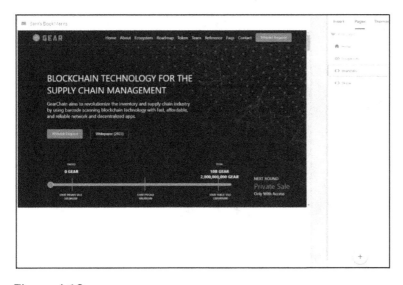

Figure 4.10

You can add a website as a link or include the entire site as Full page content in your google site. It's convenient to embed websites because you can see the entire site from your google sites. Note that not all website URLs can be embedded as full page content. In this case, you can utilize the iframe html codes.

As you add more favorite websites, you may want to change the navigation mode to 'Side', so you can list all of your saved sites and navigate them easily.

Figure 4.11

Figure 4.12

Testimonial Design on Google Sites: A Simple Hack

When consumers have a plethora of choices at their fingertips, trust and credibility become paramount for businesses. When someone visits your website, you have just a few seconds to capture their attention and convince them that your product or service is worth their time and money. One of the best ways to capture this is via testimonials.

How to Create an Appealing Testimonial Design

Once you've collected testimonials from your customers, the next step is to integrate them into a visually appealing design. While you can hire a designer or opt for paid widgets, you can also create an attractive design without spending a dime. Here are two options to consider:

Option 1: Convert Google Slides to Images and Create a Carousel

The simplest method is to utilize Google Slides. Assuming you already have a blank testimonial design, insert an image into the slide and add text. Then, go to "File" > "Download" and select PNG, JPG, or SVG to convert the slide into an image. Finally, you can embed it into Google Sites using the Image Carousel feature.

Figure 4.13

Here's an example of a blank testimonial image, and you can find a sample (https://tinyurl.com/sitestestimonials1)

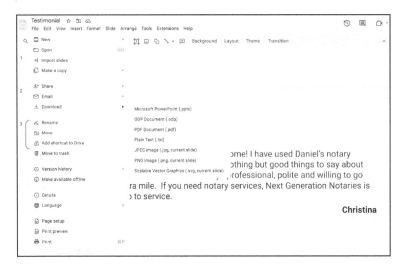

Figure 4.14

Here's how to convert Google Slides into an image.

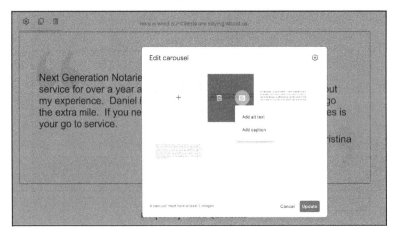

Figure 4.15

Don't forget to add alt text for SEO purposes!

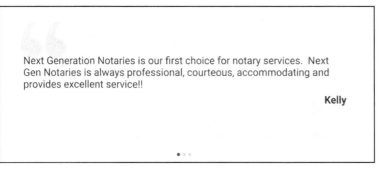

Figure 4.16

Your testimonials will look something like this when integrated into Google Sites.

Option 2: Use Widgets with a Simple Script

Another approach is to employ scripts and embed the code directly into your Google Sites. For instance, you can effortlessly embed this code:

```
<link href="https://fonts.googleapis.com/css?family=Lato&display=swap"
rel="stylesheet">
<style>
p{
border-radius:20px;
padding:20px;
color:royalblue;
background-color:f0f0f8;
font-size:14px;
font-family: 'Lato', cursive;
text-align:left;
}
</style>
<p>
- Kelly
<br><br>
```

"Vivamus sagittis lacus vel augue laoreet rutrum faucibus dolor auctor. Vestibulum id ligula porta felis euismod semper. Cras justo odio dapibus facilisis sociis natoque penatibus."

</p>

Figure 4.17

Embed this code snippet using the embed option.

Figure 4.18

You can customize various aspects such as background color and font style to suit your preferences.

That's it! With these methods, your Google Sites will shine with beautifully designed testimonials. Happy designing!

How to make LinkTree on Google Sites

What is Linktree? Linktree is a landing page service that provides a list of links to all your social media accounts, websites, and brands.

Linktree allows you to create a custom and diversified web page full of important links to share with your clients. It's free, but you must pay for extra features like adding SEO meta tags, connecting to Google Analytics, and changing the background photos.

For example, you can build something like this for free and share the link. (https://linktr.ee/googlesitestemplates)

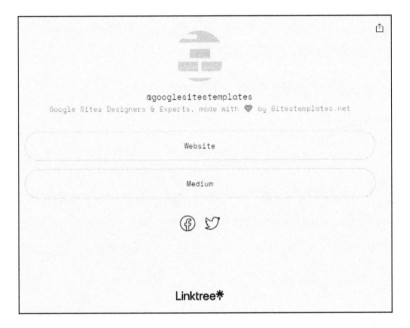

Figure 4.19

However, it may cause you trouble with phishing from scammers. For example, someone can create a Linktree page with your brand name and add links with phishing websites. Plus, you don't want to pay for paid service on Linktree in order to get additional features like SEO as mentioned above.

You can create your own Linktree page using Google Sites. The final outcome would be as follows (http://linktree.sitestemplates.net/):

Figure 4.20

You can create something similar by creating a new page or site in Google Sites. Then, mouse hover over to the right sidebar and click on 'Insert > Social Links' to add social network icons and links. Make sure to include 'alt text' for SEO purposes.

Figure 4.21

Also, you can change or add themes to your sites. You don't have to pay anything to change or add themes to your sites.

Figure 4.22

Once you complete your design, you can add this site to your domain.

Figure 4.23

That's it! You've just created your own Linktree in Google Sites and you can now promote this page to your partners, clients, or anyone else.

How to Use Email Marketing for Google Sites

According to Startup Marketing Research, 41.3% of startups don't have a digital marketing strategy. How do you get people to visit your website? You send them an email. Email marketing has been around for decades, but it has become even more popular in recent years with the development of internet access and smartphones. With email marketing, you can build your brand's visibility among thousands of potential customers for little or no cost at all. The following are some tips on how to use email marketing for Google Sites.

What is Email Marketing?

Email marketing is a form of advertising that can be used to promote a company or product. It's an inexpensive and easy way to reach potential customers. With email, you can customize your message and send it directly to people who might be interested in what you offer. Email marketing is growing because people are constantly on their smartphones, checking their email constantly.

The benefits of email marketing are enormous. It's an effective way to reach potential customers because they are always available for emails. They are cheap to produce, so anyone can afford them — even smaller companies or entrepreneurs with limited funds for their business.

They're easy to design, too, if you know how to create HTML mail. And there are countless ways to use them — from sending coupons or e-books as incentives for the customer to buy your product or service, to sending notifications about upcoming events at your store or office!

Why Use Email Marketing?

Email marketing is an easy way to keep in contact with your customers without taking too much of their time. It also has the advantage of being inexpensive and effective for businesses of all sizes.

The best part of email marketing is that you can choose when people will receive your message. For example, you can send out a short email with information about a new product on your website each week. When people are looking for what you have to offer, they will be more likely to visit your site if they see these emails pop up in their inbox on a regular basis.

You can also use email marketing to let customers know about sales or specials on products they've shown interest in before. Whatever kind of message you want to send, email marketing will get it across while still giving people the opportunity to unsubscribe if they don't want to hear from you anymore.

In a nutshell:

- Email marketing is a cost-effective way to promote your business: It doesn't require any expense, and it can be done by anyone.

- You can target an unlimited number of people with email marketing: With this method, you'll know that your message will reach the right people on all devices.

- You don't need to create a website for customers to visit: If you've been thinking about creating a website but haven't had time, email marketing gives you the opportunity to get your brand out there.

- Email marketing is easy and doesn't take a lot of time: With email marketing, you don't have to invest in expensive ads or market research. All it takes is sending a short message to potential customers using your digital contact list.

- It's cheap and easy to measure results: You can provide tracking links in your messages so that you can find out which emails are clicked on the most by recipients. This information will allow you to change up your strategy accordingly.

Add Subscription Marketing for Google Sites

Email subscription marketing is one of the most cost-effective ways to promote your product or service. If you have a list of people who have asked for your information, this is a great way to get in touch with them and let them know about your latest news.

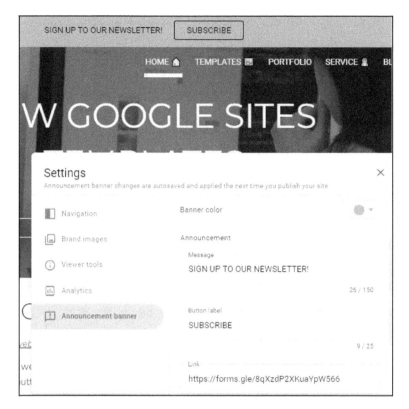

Figure 4.24

Step 1. Create a list of your contacts

The first step to email marketing is to create a list of all the email addresses you plan to send ads to. This should be a select group of people who have shown interest in your product or service and would be willing to receive information from you about your business. The more relevant the contact, the better chance you have of generating revenue from those emails. Additionally, you may want to build a subscriber list on your Google Sites. Using a google form, a name and email can be collected, and the form can be incorporated into the announcement bar.

Step 2. Send out emails regularly

Once you've created a list of contacts, it's time to start sending out emails on a regular basis. The volume and frequency with which you mail depends on your budget and how often your company communicates with clients.

Some companies send out promotional emails every week, others send them monthly, and some only communicate through email when they're announcing something new or significant.

Step 3. Make sure your subject line captures attention

Your subject line is one of the most important parts of the email because it can determine whether or not somebody opens it or not. When crafting an eye-catching subject line, make sure it's concise, but impactful enough to capture attention and make somebody curious about what's inside.

An email marketing tool like Constant Contact or Mailchimp can be useful. Moreover, you can hire professional email template designers and delegate email marketing campaigns as well.

Convert Your Google Sites into Pitch Deck

Your Google Sites can be a great tool for presenting your pitch deck. Yes, Microsoft PowerPoint slides and google slides already offer this, and you can build pitch deck slides and share them with a link. However, there are two major drawbacks in PowerPoints and Google Slides.

To start with, all Google Slides links begin with docs.google.com, which is a very long URL. Take a look at this slide URL, for example. The link is too long, so the recipient may hesitate to open it, thinking it is a phishing or invalid link. Besides, your brand hardly reflects this link.
https://docs.google.com/presentation/d/1nbyiMVTmMqL04lIuoj1sxnySPeELmeUd79__IPz7i0U/edit?usp=sharing

Although you can use short URL services like tinyurl, it still starts with their brand name. In addition, analytics cannot be used to monitor traffic. Analyzing traffic sources and further targeting based on analytics insights is important if you are promoting material for public audiences.

All of these can be achieved with Google Sites. You can build a perfect pitch deck in Google Sites without sacrificing your slide design.

Create Your Google Sites for Pitch Deck

The first thing you need to do is create a new Google Site. Start with any template or a blank Google Sites template if you prefer.

On the right sidebar, click the plus circle under the 'Page' menu pane. Here, you will find four options. Choose 'Full page embed'.

Figure 4.25

Now you will see two options: Add embed and Add from Drive.

Figure 4.26

If you click the 'Add embed' option, you can embed your pitch deck file or design from your script code or site link.

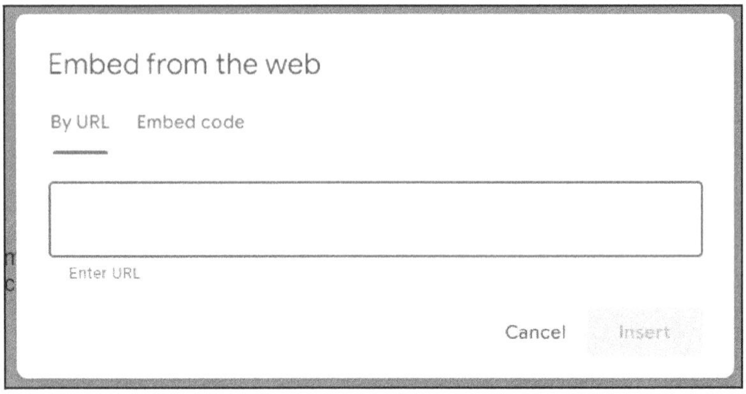

Embed from the web
By URL
Embed code
Enter URL
Cancel
Insert

Figure 4.27

The simplest option is to click 'Add from Drive'. You can choose your pitch deck from your google drive and it will appear like this. To share your pitch deck slides with others, make sure the sharing option is set to 'anyone with the link can view'.

SITES TEMPLATES
Company Name
Pitch Deck

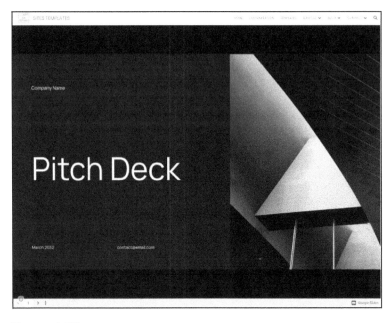

Figure 4.28

Customize Your Pitch Deck in Google Sites

The logo and menu navigation bar can be removed so your pitch deck appears full screen if you don't want them to be visible.

You will also notice three icons, including gear, when you mouse hover over the pitch deck area in Google Sites. Using the gear icon, you can adjust presentation settings such as AutoStart, look playback, delay time per slide, and starting slide number.

Figure 4.29

Add a domain and Google analytics for branding.

The next step is to align your Google Sites-based deck with your brand. Your pitch deck will display with your brand or company's domain instead of the default Google sites URL at sites.google.com.

As an example, here is the sample pitch deck for this demo:
https://www.sitestemplates.net/pitch-demo

Your next step is to embed your Google Analytics to your website after adding a domain to your Google sites. In this way, you can track your website traffic and gain insight into your visitors.

Sign up for Google Analytics with your Google account if you do not already have it. Create a new property and enter the website address that you want to track under the 'data stream' menu. And you will see the MEASUREMENT ID which is the tracking ID.

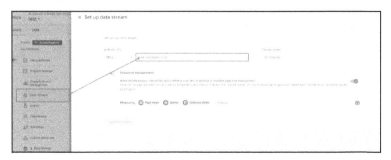

Figure 4.30

On your Google Sites, click the gear icon on the top menu bar and paste your Google Analytics code. For further information on setting up Google Analytics, click the 'Learn more' link on the screenshot below.

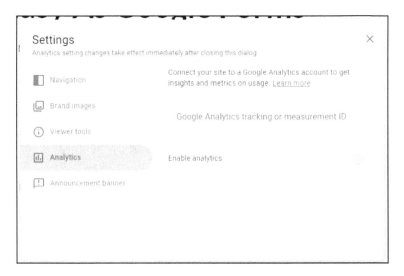

Figure 4.31

Advanced: Get track record specifically for targeted campaigns.

If you want to track your campaign specifically, you can create a campaign URL.

Suppose you want to share your pitch deck website link with a specific community, online advertising or subscribers.

Visit Campaign URL Builder (https://ga-dev-tools.web.app/campaign-url-builder/) website and you can make a url something like this:
https://www.sitestemplates.net/pitch-demo?utm_source=newsletter&utm_medium=email&utm_campaign=2023

How to download images and HTML files from Google Sites for website migration.

When it comes to google sites, you may need to know how to get the site downloaded in order for you to be able to use it on various platforms. Depending on your site's version, there are ways that can help with downloading all of the files and images within your website.

How to Export Classic Google Sites

If you have classic google sites, you can utilize Classic Sites Manager(https://sites.google.com/classicsitesmanager) to download them. Visit the Classic Site Manager page and choose a site that you wish to download. Just click the "download" button on this page to export.

Figure 4.32

How to Export New Google Sites

If you have a new Google site, you can use the Google Takeout tool, which allows you to download your entire Google services in one go.

You can download your Google Sites by going to Google Drive and searching for your Google Sites type.

Figure 4.33

Side Note: You'll notice your new Google Sites doesn't consume any space in your Google Drive, but once you export the files, you'll be surprised to learn the actual file size on your computer.

Next, create a new folder, let's say 'My Google Sites' and drag your website files into it. Then, go to Google Takeout > Select only 'Google Drive' > Select 'Advanced settings' and select 'My Google Sites' folder, and then click the next button at the bottom of the page.

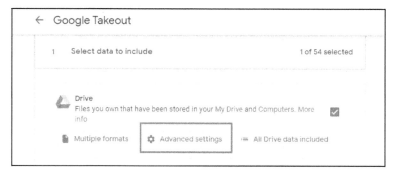

Figure 4.34

Figure 4.35

You will be prompted to enter your Gmail password. That's it! You will be notified via email once the website export is completed.

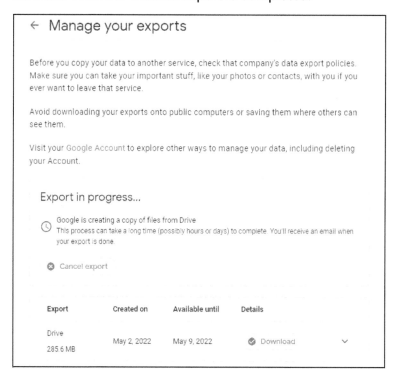

Figure 4.36

Click the download button to begin downloading the compressed file. All of your Google Sites files-including HTML, images, and more-can be found in the compressed file.

Host Your Google Sites on Firebase and Make It as an App

Google Firebase (http://firebase.google.com/) is an application development platform that makes it easy to build web applications and apps. With Google Sites, you can build a free website by using the sites.google.com URL and adding your own domain.

Unlike other zero-coding website builder platforms such as Wix, Google Sites can be exported and downloaded as HTML files and hosted under Google Firebase.

Why do you want your Google sites to be hosted in Firebase? There will be lots of use cases, such as making a better website. Apart from that, you can do lots of other things such as A/B testing, expand to applications, etc. You can also host your images with a permanent URL.

Google Firebase is basically free for up to a certain usage tier, so it will give you another way to promote your online presence.

Step 1. Export Google Sites as HTML files

First step is to download your Google Sites and export as HTML. Using Google Takeout, you can export only a specific Google Site. Extract the zip file into your computer's folder after you download it.

Step 2. Install programming tools

You will need to install Visual Studio Code (https://code.visualstudio.com/), Node JS (https://nodejs.org/), Firebase-CLI (https://firebase.google.com/docs/cli) before you can launch your website on Firebase

Step 3. Create a Firebase project

Visit Google Firebase, sign in with your Gmail account. Click to create a new project and enter your project name.

Figure 4.37

You can add Google Analytics by enabling it and clicking continue.

Figure 4.38

You will be asked to log in to Google Analytics and choose a property or create a new one.

Figure 4.39

Step 4. Add Firebase to your website and deploy

The next step is to create a project. You can set up a firebase hosting and register the app.

Figure 4.40

After copying this entire firebase SDK script, go to the folder where you have extracted the Google Sites HTML file. Launch the Visual Studio Code in this directory, open your homepage file and paste it before </body> tab. In this example, I did it on my HOME.html file.

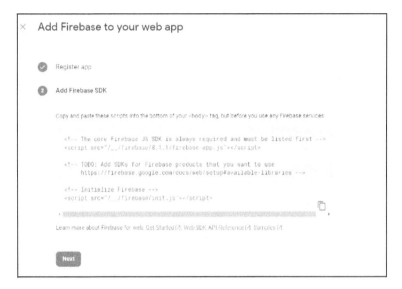

Figure 4.41

Figure 4.42

Now the next step is to install Firebase CLI if you haven't done that. After that, deploy the firebase hosting. You can launch a terminal in Visual Studio Code and enter 'firebase login' > 'firebase init' > You would need to choose 'hosting' options. It will ask you to create a 'public' folder by default. Continue by typing y.

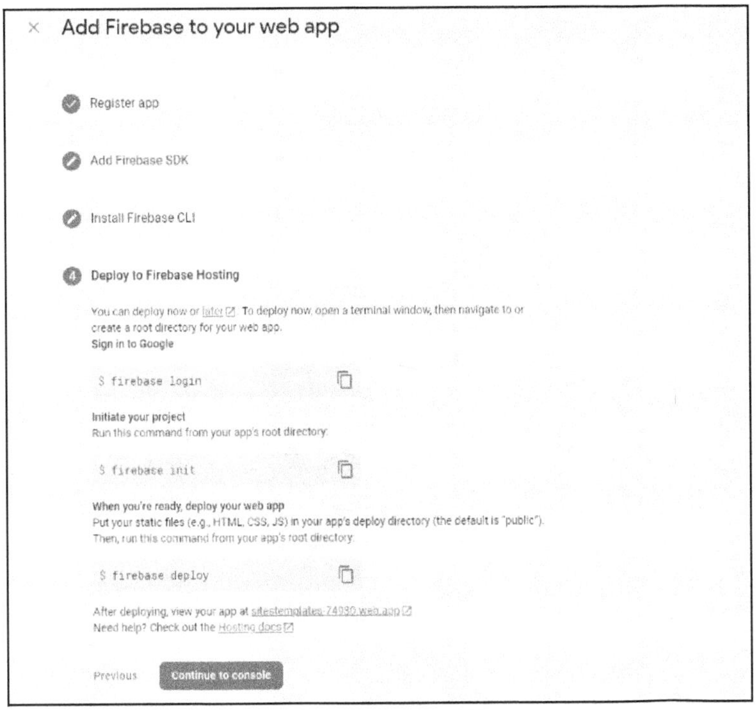

Figure 4.43

After initiation is complete, you will notice that a public folder is created. Now comes the important part, make sure to move all the files and folders under the public folder.

Figure 4.44

After that enter 'firebase deploy' It will then deploy your entire files in the public folder into the firebase.

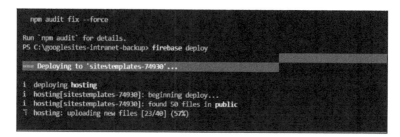

Figure 4.45

Once completed, your entire website will look like this under Firebase. Mission accomplished! You can find the google sites in Firebase hosting. For example, https://sitestemplates-74930.web.app/HOME.html

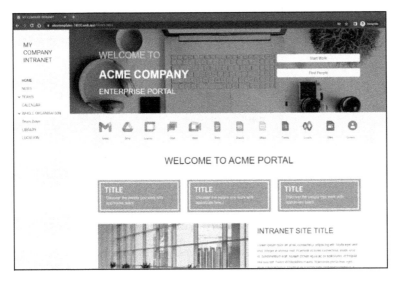

Figure 4.46

CHAPTER 5 Other Useful Resources

Get the Most Out of Google Business Profile Manager

Google Business Profile Manager makes it easier than ever for businesses to keep track of their Google business profile information from one location. That means you no longer need to keep track of separate Google business account URLs, phone numbers, and email addresses for each of your businesses. Instead, you can manage all of your business's Google business profile information from one single location.

This is a great time to check your Google business profile information to make sure your business information is up to date, and ensure you're getting the most out of Google's numerous features for local businesses. Here are some tips to get you started with Google Business Profile Manager.

Set up Google Business Profile Manager

Google Business Profile Manager is available for businesses to use for free. To start using it, you first have to set up your Google business profile. Once you do, go to the new Google Business Profile Manager and sign in with your existing Google business account or create a new one. Once there, you'll be given access to manage all of your Google business profile information from one location.

Figure 5.1

Check your Google business profile

The first thing you should do with Google Business Profile Manager is to check your Google business profile. One of the most important things you'll want to make sure is that all of your information, including phone numbers and addresses, are still up-to-date.

Use Keywords and DFID to Rank Better in Google

The best way to update your SEO is to use the Keywords and Description fields on Google Business Profile Manager to include keywords that are relevant to the services or products you offer. These keywords will help your business rank higher in Google searches for those terms, which could help increase traffic to your website.

Build a Landing Page; it's similar to Google Sites

Google Business Profiles gives you a website builder that is similar to Google Sites. You can easily build one page websites or landing pages for your business without needing a domain name. The default website address will be like yoursitename.business.site

Figure 5.2

Promotions, Offers, Events and New posts

You can take advantage of "Posts" to make the most out of Google Maps listings. With discounts, promotional offers, events and blog posts highlighted on your listing, this is a great opportunity for you to showcase what your company does!

Figure 5.3

Track your Reviews and Ratings

Google Business Profile Manager makes it easy for you to keep track of your reviews and ratings. You can also view how your ratings have changed over time.

This is a great way to get a gauge on how your customers are interacting with your business.

Bing's Image Creator: Using AI to Create Stunning Images

Creating visual content that stands out is crucial for individuals and businesses alike. Fortunately, with the help of artificial intelligence (AI), generating high-quality images has never been easier. Bing's Image Creator is a tool that leverages AI to enable users to create stunning images effortlessly. In this article, we'll dive into how to use Bing's Image Creator and discuss the copyright protection of AI-created images.

Using Bing's Image Creator

To start using Bing's Image Creator, navigate to the Bing Image search page and click on "Image Creator" located in the top menu bar. You'll be taken to a page where you can input your desired image idea or concept. Once you've entered your search term, click "Create" and you will get four different images. Note that you need to have a Microsoft account in order to use this service.

Explore ideas and surprise me

Another cool feature of Image Creator is that you can get an idea of images or get totally surprised by stunning images by clicking surprise me button. This will give you some idea on designing and finding best images for your site themes.

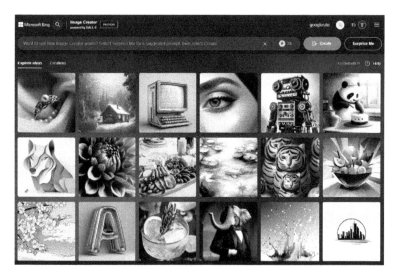

Figure 5.4

Copyright Protection of AI-Created Images

One question that often arises when using AI to create images is whether they are copyright protected. According to Bing's Image Creator Terms and Conditions, you can use it for any legal, personal, non-commercial purpose.

Gamify Your Google Sites with Games

One of the great features of Google Sites is the ability to embed games directly into your site. This means that you can share your favorite games with your visitors without having to redirect them to another website.

One website that has successfully embedded Games into their Google Sites page is Google Doogle Games website. This Google Sites has nearly 50K monthly traffic and provides an enjoyable way to play some of the most popular Google Doodle games.

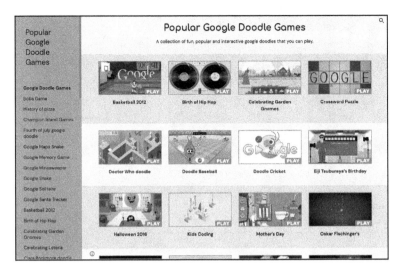

Figure 5.5

By incorporating gamification into your website, you can enhance the overall experience for your visitors. One way to achieve this is by utilizing the 'Full Page Embed' feature, which allows you to embed a flash game. As an example, you can visit the test website provided and view the game after watching a 15-second advertisement. https://www.sitestemplates.net/test-game

Figure 5.6

"Spin to Win" is another great way to gamify your website and give a pleasant experience with rewards to your visitors. You can embed via embed function on Google Sites.

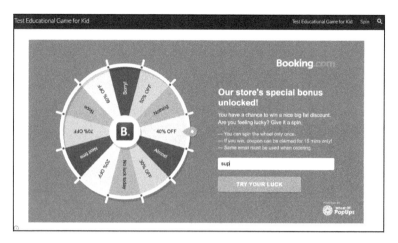

Figure 5.7

Please keep in mind that the above examples are solely for demonstration purposes for the blog and we do not intend to promote particular games or infringe on any copyrights.

It is important to note that Google Sites has its own program policies, and if your website violates these terms, your site and/or your accounts may be suspended or deleted. So before embedding any games or content into your Google Sites page, make sure to read and follow the terms and conditions carefully.

Considerations When Choosing A Designer For Your Google Sites.

After the recent launch of Google Sites, many people are looking for someone to help them create a website. But don't worry, here are six considerations if you absolutely need a designer on your team if you want to be successful.

Benefits of having Designers onboard for your project.

1. Your website will look professional

A great designer can help you create a website that looks good and also incorporates your company's branding. Even if you don't have a lot of experience with design or know what makes a good layout, it should be easy to find someone to help you who does.

2. It's less expensive than hiring someone to do everything

If you don't know how to code and would like for your website to do more than just display text, then designers are the way to go. Designers are skilled at building websites from scratch, from copying templates, or from editing pre-existing ones. Designers usually charge by the hour instead of a flat price for their services which may end up being cheaper in the long run. You'll also need someone to write SEO-friendly content and optimize your site for conversions if you want it to perform well on Google search engine results pages (SERPs).

3. It's easier for them to make changes

Designers are experts at designing websites and making changes as needed once it's live online, so they'll have an easier time handling these tasks than if you were trying to learn how yourself. They're also better versed in what to do.

6 Reasons You Need a Designer

If you're reading this book, I'm guessing you've contemplated building your own website. But even if you are comfortable with building a site yourself or have considered hiring an in-house web designer, there are some good reasons to hire a professional Google Sites designer too.

Building a website can be time consuming and expensive. Not to mention the fact that many people lack the expertise to create a professional looking site. But if you are determined to build your own site, it's important that you are aware of these six reasons why designers are necessary for success.

1. Designers have the tools, knowledge, and experience needed for improving your site. Hiring someone who specializes in web design will allow them to offer input on the content, as well as the design and layout.

2. Designers ensure you're creating the best user experience.

3. Designers will make sure your site is responsive on all devices.

4. Designers will make sure you're meeting the Google Search Essentials (formerly Webmaster Guidelines) at https://developers.google.com/search/docs/advanced/guidelines/webmaster-guidelines

5. Designers make sure your Google site is easy to update with new content.

6. Hiring a web designer means that they'll have ample time to work on your project and you can focus on being creative with your business.

Bonus for Our Readers.

- 10% OFF on any Google Workspace plans
- 10% OFF on Dropbox Business plans
- One free Google Sites templates from sitestemplates.com

Visit https://tinyurl.com/masteringgooglesites and enter the coupon code "MASTER"

ABOUT THE AUTHOR

Harry has been a Google Sites expert for over a decade, and his experience has enabled him to create intricate and comprehensive webpages. He also manages the Google Sites Facebook community and blog posts, ensuring visitors learn with enjoyment. His proficiency and mastery with Google Sites has been immensely beneficial to readers in creating engaging and successful websites, as well as conforming to the most recent trends in Google. He facilitates individuals to exploit the potential of current tech, such as cloud computing, IT-driven marketing and web3 blockchain, to the fullest. He currently lives in San Jose, California with his family.

Website: http://www.sitestemplates.net
Facebook: https://www.facebook.com/googlesitesdesign
Twitter: https://twitter.com/sitestemplates
Linkedin: https://www.linkedin.com/in/harryjung/